At long last... the TRUE Customarily Derbyshire

Dafydd Manton

Published by Heron Publications Ltd, 2011.

Copyright Dafydd Manton & Heron Publications, 2011.

www.heronpublications.co.uk

www.dafydd-manton.co.uk

Dafydd Manton has asserted his right under the Copyright, Designs and Patents Act 1988 to be identified as the author of this work.

This book is sold subject to the condition that it shall not, by way of trade or otherwise, be lent, resold, hired out or otherwise circulated without the publisher's prior consent in any form other than that in which it is published.

First published in 2011 by Heron Publications Ltd,
24 Hutcliffe Wood Road, Beauchief, Sheffield, S8 0EX.
Telephone: 0114 2357777

info@heronpublications.co.uk

ISBN 978-0-9564825-1-8

Typeset and Designed by Heron Publications Ltd.

Printed and bound by Printability, Concept House, Westwick Park, Broombank Road, Chesterfield, S41 9QJ

Ann Manton

Illustrations

Dafydd Manton: p14, 18, 21, 23, 26, 34, 39, 41, 45, 76, 85, 99, 103, 105, 108, 111, 113, 116.

Ann Manton: p11, 48, 58, 66, 89.

Jess Clark: p82.

Photographs: Mike Firth.

Contents

Sticking With Tradition 6

Alport Love Feast 7

Ashbourne Highland Gathering 9

Ashbourne Shrovetide Football 13

Bakewell Pudding 17

Baslow Church Clock Face 20

Bradwell Ice Cream 22

Bonsall Hen Racing 25

Brailsford Ploughing Match 28

Castleton Garland 30

Chapel-en-le-Frith Curfew Bell 33

Chesterfield Crooked Spire 36

Chesterfield Market 40

Coal Aston Hook and Hoop 42

Creswell Crags Artwork 44

Derby & Bonnie Prince Charlie 47

Derby Florentine Boar 50

Derby Ram 52

Derby Tup 55

Derbyshire Cheese 57

Derbyshire Dry Stone Walls 59

Derbyshire Executions 61

Derbyshire Highwaymen 64

Derbyshire Morris Dancing 67

Derbyshire Mummers & Guisers 70

Derbyshire Passing The Posset 73

Derbyshire Punishments 75

Eyam & The Plague 78

Flagg Races 80

Grindon Hedgehog Rolling 83

Hayfield May Queen 86

Longshaw Sheepdog Trials 88

Matlock Bath Venetian Nights 92

Pikehall Harness Racing 95

Stainsby Festival 98

Tissington Well Dressings 101

Tunstead Dickey 104

Weston-on-Trent Scarecrows 107

Wetton Toe Wrestling 109

Winster Pancake Races 112

Wirksworth Barmote Courts 115

Wirksworth Church Clipping 118

Miscellaneous Traditions 121

Conclusion 124

Meet The Author 126

Sticking With Tradition

It is customary for books to offer their readers an introduction. A publication about customs just dare not step out of line, so here it is.

SO what exactly is a custom or tradition? It is something that has happened for a long time, having started for a reason, however obscure, and is likely to go on for some considerable time yet.

Frankly, we haven't got a clue why most traditions began, except that there were some people with very little to do on a dark winter's night, and candles at twopence a dozen, so they used their imagination. Pagan religion often plays a part, but then again, it was something else to do, in the absence of the Nine O'Clock News. Not much changes.

To illustrate, if you were to read that the local tradition of aardvark buttering, started last year by Mr Len Wormwood, is to be discontinued due to a lack of aardvarks, you wouldn't think much of it as a tradition, and that it was merely a passing fad.

By the same token, some things are widespread, but hardly a custom - the use of Tupperware, for example. At one time, husbands would customarily beat their wives, which was even sanctioned under law as far back as 782 AD. Indeed, the expression "Rule of Thumb" is thought by some to quantify the size of the stick, no thicker than a man's thumb, with which he could "correct" his wife.

"What time is it, dear?" he asked

"Just gone six, my love. Why?"

"It's nearly time for your beating."

"Oh, right. Shall I go and get your stick then, and afterwards we'll have a nice hot cup of tea? Fancy a chocolate digestive with it?"

Not really a custom, although it is nice that the law has ever been so thoughtful as to the welfare of the ordinary citizen.

Customs are not just important, but vital. They are the lifeblood of any community, whether it is rural or urban, for all of our urban settlements were rural once. But, perhaps most importantly of all - and this is worth bearing in mind as you read further - is that they are traditional.

Alport Love Feast

It is not the kind of love where you go up to someone and give them a hug, although it isn't necessarily out of the question.

IF you're going to San Francisco, be sure to wear some flowers in your hair. If you're going to San Francisco you're gonna meet some gentle people there. This is because, in the Hippy era, which was a source of much merriment to many on the outside, the in-thing was a love-in.

It was a soup of magic mushrooms, free love, Joan Baez and Bob Dylan, long hair, people making strange "Peace" signs with their fingers a mode de Winston Churchill's "Victory" sign, strange multi-coloured clothing which hid the beer/wine/egg/gravy stains, and staring in to the middle distance for hours on end, whilst the mind wandered free. Like. Man.

Therefore, when you see the phrase "Love Feast" in your local newspaper, you could be forgiven for rushing upstairs and looking out the loon-pants, sandals and tie-dyed T-shirt. Oh, and throwing the deodorant away. This is, I regret to tell you, slightly misleading.

In the first instance, look on the bright side - it saves you having to remember all those dreary protest songs, whereby the assumption was that the men in the suits, or the men in the tanks, were going to take any notice of the people with the heart-shaped, pink glasses and the acoustic guitars. The average tank driver would quite happily have shoved it in to gear and gone right through the middle! In a battle between a small wooden guitar and a Chieftain tank weighing in at 55 tons, there are no prizes for guessing who would win. Having said that, it would be a pretty shoddy way of declaring your love for somebody, although you might claim that it had a thick edge over some of the music from that time.

No, the Love Feast is a Methodist festival, held on the first Sunday in July at Alport. It is a very simple affair, which takes place in a barn, with straw on the floor, and rudimentary seating. The communion bread and wine are changed for fruitcake and water, which rather flies in the face of Scripture, but who are we to argue? Jesus used unleavened bread for a reason, referring to the "leaven of the Pharisees", meaning corruption, so to replace it with something with currants, cherries and sultanas does seem a bit odd. Possibly even corrupt.

However, John Wesley claimed it had "apostolicity", although there is no reference to a slice of Dundee, or a chunk of Stollen anywhere in the gospels. There are also claims that the cake and water have no symbolic meaning at all, so we might as well admit that we're all confused.

The water is passed from person to person in a two-handled loving cup, which fits rather nicely. The hymns are unaccompanied, which doubtless sounds wonderful. The practice goes back more than 240 years, to the early days of Methodism, when, in an act of Christian Love, they were being persecuted.

The history of the churches was ever thus; nobody remembers the Spanish Inquisition fondly, and it is unlikely that Thomas a Becket was thrilled to be stabbed in the grounds of Canterbury Cathedral. This is where we get the song "There's a Hole in my Becket".

The history of the Love Feast, which you would hope is all sweetness and light, has been a long catalogue of arguments, fights, near punch-ups, drunkenness and general squabbling. It was not a new idea either, because the festival went back to the year 407 AD, when it was known as the Agape (pronounced 'a garp ay') Feast, Agape being the Greek word for love, in the sense of Principled love, or, if you prefer, love with obligations to others.

It is not the kind of love where you go up to someone and give them a hug, although it isn't necessarily out of the question. It's just that if you chose the wrong person, you might well end up copping for a bunch of fives up the bracket - another expression you won't find in the Gospels.

The love feasts were first practised in England, courtesy of John Wesley, in 1738. It was, at that time, an all male affair, which seems a bit mean, but then they had one just for the women. It seems a bit unnecessary nowadays, since we are a more integrated society. It is also difficult to imagine a whole bunch of 18th century Methodists ogling each other, half way up a hillside in a 50mph gale, whilst the hymns are being sung.

The bit I like best is, though, that entry was by ticket only, and initially only to those who could attest to their salvation. Hmmmm. I'm sure they didn't do that at the feeding of the 5,000; you'll remember that bit about five loaves and two fishes. Better yet, there were some who slipped in without tickets, which conjures up pictures of touts standing just down the road and muttering out of the corner of their mouths, "Ere, Guv, wanna buy a ticket for a bit of cake and a cup of water - only 'alf a nicker to you! Prayers 'alf a crown extra!"

It seems fair to say that religion in England in the 18th century was a minefield, and there is no better illustration of that fact than a paper written by one Gregory Oldknow (a name you could have hours of fun with) of Spondon. The snappy little title of said paper was "A Serious Objection To The Pernicious Doctrines of the Moravians and Methodists", dated 1751. In this carefully reasoned, informed, balanced and judicious document, the esteemed Mr Oldknow pointed out that the Methodists were pickpockets, cannibals, and the intention of their Love Feasts was to squeeze money out of the poor.

Obviously, he must have had ample evidence for these claims, such as having had his pocket picked my someone with a label round their neck saying "John Wesley Rools OK", or having had his granny eaten. Sadly, we will never know. But he records worse calumnies yet, and if you are of a nervous disposition, please look away now. He tells a waiting world of the fact that at some Feasts they played the bass viol, and at others not, thus proving that they were unsteady in their minds, and therefore a Danger to the Church and State.

Visit Alport at your peril. If you want to know where to go, listen for the bass viol. Or not. Just don't eat anybody on the way, that's all. They'll only pick your pocket.

Ashbourne Highland Gathering

There was a surplus of telegraph poles when the railways did not go as far as originally planned and they were lying around the place.

A NOSTRIL is a fairly small orifice. The blade of a claymore, the traditional Highland sword, is about 35 inches in length. Say anything to upset a Highlander and he will possibly be tempted to find out how much of that nearly a yard of cold steel will fit up the average nose, especially if that nose happens to be English.

The answer is, not very much, before the eyes start to water, and that is not the eyes of the sword-bearer, it is the eyes either side of the offending nose, which is directly above the offending mouth, which started all this in the first place.

That being the case, this chapter will not, at any time, attempt to take the mickey out of the Scots and their wonderful heritage, which they so very kindly bring south to Ashbourne.

If you wish to get all this in to perspective, the Black Watch, probably the most famous of all the Highland regiments, were nicknamed the "Ladies from Hell" by crack German troops, who were totally in awe of these ferocious fighting men in kilts. If the Highlanders are not going to quail at several thousand German Guardsmen, it would be folly to antagonise anybody now.

So, why does a town in Derbyshire have a Highland Gathering, since it is a goodly distance from Scotland? Well, believe it or not, Ashbourne founded a pipe band in 1976, the original purpose of which was to play for pleasure. Now, it is worth bearing in mind that the pipes are specifically designed to make the men fight better in wartime, and also to put fear into the enemy. However, there is no enemy at such an event, which means that the pipes will either make you want to start a punch-up, or run away from one. Since this happens on a ratio of exactly one-to-one, actual fights are very rare, since everybody is going in a different direction.

As you would imagine, a Highland Gathering contains all the elements of a similar event in Scotland, only held a bit further south. You couldn't have one without caber-tossing, hammer-throwing, bagpipes, haggis, porridge and whisky. In fairness, you could get rid of the caber-tossing, the hammer-throwing, the pipes, haggis and porridge, but some things are sacrosanct. One of the reasons that Scotsmen wear the kilt is that, after a night on the Glen-Fallingover it is practically impossible to find individual trouser legs, much less zips, so this is a very practical move indeed.

Similarly, trying to find your keys/fags/aspirin/mobile in a pocket is quite hard, especially as you can't peer into it, but a sporran is relatively free-moving, and can, if necessary, be brought up to bloodshot eye-level, and ferreted in.

The little dagger carried in the sock is useful for getting into tins, cleaning the fingernails, acting as surrogate eating irons, or for cutting loose ill-fitting sporrans. As an offensive weapon, it is practically worse than useless, since Scotsmen are usually not very tall, therefore do not have especially long legs, therefore have less space for daggers than the average Amazon.

The only part of Highland garb that defies reason is the use of tartan, since it is useless as camouflage, expensive to make and hurts the eyes first thing in the morning, particularly after the night before. Tradition has it that it is to do with recognition of individual tribes, but since they all look much the same from a distance, and if you've
got close enough to realise that you are faced by an enemy tartan, you're in deep trouble. It is of much less use than a helmet with a spike on the top of it, for example, or a busby.

There is also the point, if you will excuse the pun, that trying to remember whether blue squares with three yellow lines and two red ones is friendlier than red squares with two yellow lines and three blue ones is hard enough at the best of times. Name badges would be much easier, all things considered. Particularly in the hill race where competitors are, one hopes, moving fairly fast. Wearing numbers is far more efficient, but mundane.

How did the original Highland sports come about? Some are obvious: if you've got plenty of deer to wrestle, that is what you wrestle; there would be no point in having to specially import boar if you've already got a plethora of slightly stroppy stags.

However, the tossing of the caber is not quite so simple. Many will tell you that the caber is merely the trunk of a Scots Pine, with the branches cut off, but that is patently ridiculous, since every tree is different, never mind what the Forestry Commission might say.

What really happened was that there was a surplus of telegraph poles when the railways in Scotland did not go as far as originally planned and they were lying around the place, getting in the way. The local men, big strapping lads who had been brought up on oats and whisky, found the easiest way was to lift them, get them upright, then bung them in the local river. It also saved noise pollution from the chainsaws, so it was an environmental move.

As proof, give any small boy a body of water and something he can throw in to it, and Ladbroke's wouldn't take bets on what is going to happen next. Since the vast majority of men are still little boys at heart, what better combination could there be than telephone poles and a river?

As well as the pipes, the sports include teams of bug-eyed, sweaty men trying to pull a rope harder than another team of bug-eyed, sweaty men. One has to hope that this is not done in kilts. What is done in kilts, though, is the Highland dancing, which is a sight more complicated that it looks. Particularly so is the sword dance, which legend has it was

*Ashbourne is reputed to stage the largest
Highland Gathering outside Scotland*

performed by troops prior to battle. Custom says that if the dancer touched a sword with his foot, then he would die on the morrow, which seems to be the sort of fact you'd rather not know.

The Scottish variation is usually done with two swords forming a cross and is known as a "hilt and point" dance, and when well executed - perhaps the wrong word to use in the circumstances - is a joy to behold, dancers almost seeming to float in the air.

Curiously, whilst Ashbourne is reputed to be the largest Highland Gathering outside Scotland, it is not the only place in Derbyshire with a sword-dancing tradition. The village of Coxbench has a traditional long sword dance, which is not just a dance but a play as well. The characters in it are many and varied, being Betsy Belzebub, Devil Downt, Noble Slasher, Venture-in, Father Christmas and Doctor Prince Paradine.

It would take half a Norwegian hillside's worth of paper to try and explain the proceedings, so if you want to know more, you could either read it up in one of those terribly serious documents about Morris Dancing, for it is a form of Morris, or quite simply go and watch it. If you can't get to Coxbench, there is a similar one at Codnor. Strange to relate, it ends up with the dancers going for a drink - which comes as no shock whatsoever. The various events at Ashbourne do, as well. Nunc est bibendum?

Ashbourne Shrovetide Football

Murder or manslaughter is prohibited and the use of unnecessary violence is frowned upon. The ball must not be carried in any motorised vehicle, nor may it be hidden up coats or jumpers.

I HAVE a confession to make. Up until recently - well, about 20 minutes ago actually - I didn't know what the significance of Shrove Tuesday was. The term rarely cropped up as far as I remember, being more commonly known as Pancake Day.

This was the one day of the year when mothers the length and breadth of the country would put flour, salt, eggs, milk and butter in a bowl, and mix it until they went blue in the face. Bear in mind that was before electricity did the job for you. The fruits of their labours were then fried, tossed if you were adventurous, scraped from the ceiling if you were a bit too enthusiastic, covered with lemon juice (and this was also before the days of those little plastic lemon-shaped squirters), sprinkled with sugar and then consumed to the unmistakable sound of furring arteries.

Some covered theirs with marmalade or jam, there was chocolate spread for the decadent, Marmite for the hard case, and fishpaste for the insane. This does not imply the requirement of lunacy to eat fishpaste and pancakes, but merely for eating the fishpaste itself. Shrove Tuesday was followed by Ash Wednesday, whereby the remains of yesterday's pancakes were re-heated and burnt to a crisp, the ashes being scattered on the garden for the cat to peremptorily sniff at and then walk away with arched back.

However, many hours of research, i.e. having a quick look at Google, tells me that the word 'Shrove' refers to one who has shriven, or in other words, confessed their sins. Why only one day was chosen is a mystery, unless those who observe such things are so free of sin that once a year is enough.

One of the worst possible places for confessing your sins is lying in a cold, muddy field, with stud marks from head to toe and two broken legs and it is scant consolation moaning to yourself that this is happening all over the country. Firstly, it isn't very much, thanks to various Acts of Parliament, and secondly, as you wait for the medics, your reason is a Royal one. Not, before you start writing to Buck House, that one of the Royal Princes has mugged you, but that the traditional Shrove Tuesday football match in Ashbourne is actually known as the Royal Shrovetide Football Match.

The game is started by the ball being "turned up", at two in the afternoon, and in 1928 the turner-upperer was none other than the Prince of Wales, the future Edward VIII. In 2003, the ball was turned up by HRH the present Prince of Wales, which begs the question where the connection between Ashbourne and Wales is, unless this was just a coincidence.

Every single person who plays in the Ashbourne game, as well as being certifiably insane, lives in the town

This will be unlike a visit to any of the great clubs in football history, such as Ipswich in the east, Arsenal in the south, Manchester United in the west or Newcastle United in the north. Go to The Emirates Stadium, for the sake of argument, and you will see a collection of young men with improbable hairstyles, outlandish tattoos and unpronounceable names who, if somebody goes near to them, roll on the floor screaming, and clutching at an ankle, until the referee awards them an Oscar, and the little man with the magic sponge comes on and squeezes the magic formula of two parts hydrogen to one part oxygen on the wound.

Much of the professional game has little to do with footballing ability, but more to do with amateur dramatics. Well, it is if you can call up to £100,000 a week amateur. The game is no longer a British tradition, with players competing for the honour of their town, but is an international business. To illustrate, look at the names of Arsenal's team in 2009 -Almunia, Diaby, Sagna, Fabregas, Vermaelen, Senderos, Rosicky, Nasri, Eduardo, Gallas, van Persie, Vela and, to complete the exotic picture, Aaron Ramsey, who comes from Caerphilly in Wales. Not a Smith, nor a Jones, nor a Ramsbottom in sight.

Every single person who plays in the Ashbourne game, as well as being certifiably insane, lives in the town. Frankly, should you go to a small town in the Czech Republic, say, or Croatia, Mexico, Brazil even, it is highly unlikely that you will see football of such ferocity or duration. You could argue that this is because the English are (hem hem) eccentric, but the rest of the world has several more accurate phrases. Loony is one of them. Mad as a Hatter, a March Hare, a Box of Frogs, a Fish, a Badger, a Brush. Barking. They are not wrong.

The two teams are the Up'ards, who come from north of the River Henmore, and the Down'ards, who, would you believe, come from south of the river. The teams are not exclusively male, as per the Premiership, but mixed, which probably accounts for a few old scores being settled.

A serious jilting one year could well lead to osteopathy the following one. Oh, and there's none of this namby-pamby little 100-metre pitch. Oh no, it's three miles long, two miles wide and the town is in the middle of it.

The aim, along with the settling of scores, the giving of employ to bone-setters and bandage mongers, and the healthy expression of the innate human desire to hunt and dominate, a right load of old twaddle if ever there were one, is for the Up'ards to get the ball to Sturston Mill, whilst the Down'ards attempt to do the same at Clifton Mill, in order to tap the ball against the millstone three times. At this point the ball is goaled, and, if it is before 5pm, a new game is started with a new ball.

Don't be fooled into thinking that this is a one day event, though, since the game finishes at ten in the evening. Not a chance, for they are a hardy breed in Ashbourne and the game continues the next day, where bones new may be broken, and no doubt quantities of oxygenated haemoglobin scattered freely.

As in all well-thought-out sports, and Ashbourne has had a good few hundred years to think about it, the game possibly being Elizabethan (it is certainly recorded in 1683), the rules are wonderfully simple.

Murder or manslaughter is prohibited and the use of unnecessary violence is frowned upon. The ball must not be carried in any motorised vehicle, nor may it be hidden up coats or jumpers, inside anoraks or concealed in rucksacks. It would be pretty hard to do so with a few thousand people looking on, especially as the ball, hand-made by one John Harrison, is bigger than a standard football, brightly painted and filled with cork for when it inevitably finishes up in the river. The cork is to prevent it submerging, although a few players may well, much to the amusement of spectators. Actual drownings are rare, which, with teams numbering into the hundreds, is quite remarkable, if dull.

To stay on a bloodthirsty theme for a few seconds, there are those who would tell you that originally the game was played with a severed head, following an execution, but it would take a few remarkable coincidences to ensure a candidate for execution every Shrovetide, unless, of course, this is the Open Season for the criminal fraternity.

So, you have to ask yourself if there really is a whiff of insanity in all this? Not at all. Shrovetide Football does exactly what it says on the tin, except that the ball is very rarely kicked, being manhandled in massive hugs, or scrums, like a sort of Twickenham on amphetamines. It doesn't just happen on Shrove Tuesday. It lasts up to 16 hours, during which time no score may well happen. Mad? Insane? Merely eccentric? I have to confess, I'm in two minds.

Bakewell Pudding

There is no point in giving you the ingredients, since one of them is, it appears, a secret, and without it the dish is not Bakewell Pudding at all.

LET us get one thing straight, at the very outset. There is no such thing, despite what Mr Kipling and other industrial confectioners will tell you, as Bakewell Tart. It is Bakewell Pudding.

Oh, there's all kinds of rubbish spoken about it; claims are made by Mrs Beeton, all the usual taradiddle, but take no notice, especially if you happen to be in Bakewell. If you mention Bakewell Tart, you will either be on the end of a very crude joke, which you frankly deserved, or you will get a three-quarter-hour lecture on the history, etymology, recipe, origin and sale of this great delicacy.

Most of it is absolute poppycock, of course - folklore tends to be - but that is no reason for not trotting out the same stuff all over again, because we are never going to be able to prove it one way or the other, so we can make any claim we like. Therefore we shall.

The original pudding is claimed to have been made by happy accident. The story goes that in 1859 Mrs Greaves, the landlady of the White Horse, now called the Rutland Arms, left instructions to her cook to make a jam tart. Now, you have to bear in mind that jam tarts are the kind of things that we all show our children how to make, and they offer us all the help they can, by such things as making an appalling mess of the kitchen, and eating vast quantities of jam.

It transpires that the cook at the White Horse got it wrong, which must be nigh on impossible, and transposed the marzipan and jam, making what we now know as the Bakewell Pudding. Yet more astoundingly, she added a "Secret Ingredient", which is ever the action of the inexperienced. Well, you would, wouldn't you: "I don't know what I'm doing, so I'll shove something else in!" No doubt, that is how Rutherford split the atom, whilst merely trying to boil an egg.

The name came about because it "did bake well", an astounding happenstance, given that this was in the town with the same name, and is almost as trite as claiming that Lancashire Hotpot, despite being invented in that fair county, was discovered by a lanky lady who wore sheer stockings, and the name stuck.

Dover Sole, although fished near the famous White Cliffs is so called because the first person to try it was "bowled over" and the Bath bun has nothing to do with cities in Somerset, even though that is where it originated, but was first tried by a man up to his neck in hot, soapy water, with a loofah in his other hand.

The original Bakewell Pudding is claimed to have been made by happy accident

Of such coincidences is our language made up.

Anyway, the good Mrs Greaves, who managed to work out the recipe followed in error, recorded it and passed it on to a Mr Radford in her will, as you do. Mr Radford, generous to the end, as it were, passed it on to a Mr Bloomer, which, given the concatenation of baking terms, is rather wonderful.

Mr Bloomer's descendants, they tell us, still make the puddings, secret ingredient and all. In the meantime, one Mrs Wilson, who was the wife of a chandler and candlemaker in the town, got her, by now sticky, little mitts on the recipe, which the visiting noblemen who had consumed the original were rather fond of. Odd how it wasn't a visiting sales rep, or a coachman, but there you are.

Mrs Wilson made the puddings and then sold them from her husband's premises, which are, as everybody knows, now the Olde Original Bakewell Pudding Shoppe, olde Englishe spellynge optional.

There is, as you would expect with a story that dovetails quite so neatly, a rather large fly in the ointment, or in this case, the batter. The Pudding was also "known" to have been invented in 1820. Or 1860. Or any other time, because the Victorians' answer to Delia Smith, one Eliza Acton, had printed a book with a recipe for Bakewell Pudding in 1845, and Ben Mathews, a sort of 19th century Anthony Worral Thompson, beat her to it in 1839.

The fly is not alone, however. Records show the pudding to have been eaten at nearby Haddon Hall as early as 1563, it being the favourite dish of Lady Dorothy Vernon, who eloped that year. Incidentally, her nickname was Moll, which, with a shortening of her surname, gave us Malvern Water.

Bakewell Puddings, made to the correct, original and traditional recipe are only available from the Old Original Bakewell Pudding Shop, except, of course, for those you can buy in Bloomers, or the Bakewell Pudding Factory, although you could put all three alongside each other, and you wouldn't know the difference - mostly because there isn't one. However, every village needs its feuds, and if all three wish to proclaim to a waiting world that theirs is the only Real McCoy, who are we to argue? Maybe, a western-style shootout, with loaded foodmixers, would solve the issue.

There is no point in giving you the ingredients, since one of them is, it appears, a secret, and without it, the dish is not Bakewell Pudding at all. It is no more than some jam and pastry concoction, which would be a great disappointment. If you wish to try a proper Bakewell Pudding, your best bet is to go to Bakewell, or, if you are already there, hunt out one of the three shops mentioned above.

Those who are bothered about their waistline, their figure in general, or are looking for the healthy option, should stay at home and eat lettuce leaves. If, on the other hand, you consider that you did not fight your way to the top of the food chain just to eat rabbit fodder, Bakewell is the place for you.

Baslow Church Clock Face

Church towers have had clocks for ages,
but this one is a bit different;
it only has four numbers.

NOT much happens at Baslow. Well, not much until you try and pull out onto the main road from the little car park by the green, known locally as Goose Green, or Nether Green. This is the point at which you find out just how busy the road can be, the only difference being that at weekends there are fewer 44-ton trucks, but rather more elderly parties tootling along at 23mph, exchanging comments such as: "Look at all that traffic behind us; there must be something going on."

There are, however, one or two strange little quirks, which may be worthy of note, if only because it may come up in a pub quiz some night, and you want to be prepared.

One of the oddest things is the clock on the church. Nothing odd about that, I hear you say, as church towers have had clocks for ages, but this one is a bit different; it only has four numbers. Big deal, that's not new either, many of them only have three, six, nine and twelve. Look at my watch, it's just the same, what are you on about?

Just this - the numbers are one, seven, eight and nine. This is the point at which you might begin to think that Derbyshire folk are odder than at first thought, which may well be true, but the figures actually form the date 1897, the Diamond Jubilee of Queen Victoria. The other numbers, which are letters, spell out the word Victoria.

The only other local thing worthy of note that we need concern ourselves with is the story of Eagle Stone, at Baslow Edge. The rock is named after the pagan god Aigle who, for reasons best known to himself, had a penchant for throwing rocks around. Presumably, there wasn't much else to do in such a remote spot.

Anyway, the upshot of all this geological shenanigans is that, standing above Baslow is a rock, which looks, from at least one angle, like four granite spongecakes on top of each other, and is about 24ft high, or 6ft per sponge. Would these be rock buns?

The young men of Baslow were expected to prove their manhood, and thus their readiness for marriage. It had something to do with appeasing the witches as well, so there appear to be a few mixed metaphors in all this. Suffice it to say that there was a time in Baslow's long history when a young lady wouldn't accept the advances of a starry-eyed swain until he had ripped all his fingernails out trying to climb a rock, in order to get a better view than he would have got if he were 24ft lower.

Having said that, it still has a thick edge over computer dating.

Standing above Baslow is a rock which looks, from at least one angle, like four granite spongecakes on top of each other

Bradwell Ice Cream

Grandma had ice sent by train from Sheffield, which, given the steel industry, is about the last place on the planet you would have thought of as a supplier of cold things.

MENTION the word Bradwell, and what comes immediately to mind? It will probably be one of three things, those being hats, the Peak District village where such hats were made, or Bradwell's ice-cream - no doubt once made by people in those self-same hats.

Let us not forget, the beginnings of the ice-cream industry were not blighted by such trivia as health regulations, safety procedures or rules governing what colour plasters those in the food industry had to wear. Come to think of it, plasters hadn't been invented, which is one good reason for keeping away from Raspberry Ripple, but that's for another day.

Even if there had been such regulations, many can still remember those happy days when ice-cream was sold by men with a straw boater, a stained apron, a waxed moustache and enough botulism under his fingernails to fell the entire Brigade of Guards. And did people succumb to these things? Did they? Well, yes, by the thousand, but since nobody knew what it was, it didn't matter, you could always blame it on an "Unknown Wasting Disease", or Beri-Beri, picked up whilst on safari in Skegness.

It has been said that Bradwell's Ice Cream goes back to the earliest days of Bradwell, the village's, history, but since it was at one time the Roman Fort of Navio, which housed the First Cohort of Aquitanians, it seems unlikely. Claims of archaeological finds of third century sherds, thought to be cornet, have been made. This may, however, as shown by the value of geophysics, have been discarded some time later.

The village also has a long history of lead mining, and it has been suggested that lead miners may have favoured the cornet, since they could eat the nutritious part, known locally as "the cold bit", and leave the stem of biscuity stuff, which would obviously have been polluted with lead, but this is conjecture, based on the similar theory that the spine down the back of the Cornish Pasty is for holding on to. The connection is obscure, given that nobody has yet made an ice-cream pasty, but there is a shop in Padstow that sells disgusting things like banana and chocolate pasties, so it is just a matter of time really. Mind you, the chicken tikka and custard pasty is quite pleasant, on a cold winter's day.

Bradwell has been a centre of making hats since lead mining began in the area, not, as you would imagine, so that miners could look like city gents when out on the spree, but for protecting their heads whilst at work. The hats were known as Bradda Beavers, which was a shade cynical, since only the very wealthy could afford hats made of beaver skin. The only other people who wore beaver skin on the head were beavers, whom it suited slightly better, never mind the lack of work involved in the manufacture.

Claims of archaeological finds of third century sherds, thought to be cornet, have been made

Bradda is the dialect name for Bradwell, in much the same way as Tidza is the locals' name for Tideswell. Bradda Beavers were made of felt, which was processed to become extremely hard, by the simple expedient of heating with steam, rubbing, heating again and so forth,which caused the fibres, often wool, to separate and form a web. This became harder and harder as the process was applied and the material became thicker. It was forced over a wooden former, and eventually a hat was made. It was almost as hard as a steel helmet, water-resistant and the crown was ideal for sticking a candle to. The candle was not just a fashion statement, it provided light down in the mines, and this was before the invention of the Davy Lamp.

As you would imagine, the hat was a rudimentary form of the modern hard-hat and therefore totally unnecessary for making ice cream. There are few risks to the cranium whilst bunging together a double chocolate with hazelnuts, unless you were making it in industrial quantities and needed a three stone bag of hazelnuts lowering from the ceiling.

By one of those strange quirks of fate, the armed forces have long been looking for a material other than tin for making their battle-hats out of, because (a) it sets off magnetic mines and (b) it conducts electricity, which if you're fighting your way through somewhere with hanging cables, can spoil your entire weekend.

The Bradda Beaver was never even mentioned, which, if nothing else, tells you that no General ever came from Bradwell, or at least, not since the days of Septimus Severus, who rather favoured a silver helmet with a nice red plume. Pretty, admittedly, but not that practical.

Whilst Septimus was noted for thinking himself to be the bee's knees, he fell short in one particular aspect of his life, which is where we mere peasants score a Smartie point or two. He never, ever, throughout all recorded history, had a double chocolate and hazelnut cornet with raspberry sauce, which might be why he snuffed it at the tender age of 65, in, of all places, York. Odd, when you consider that it was the Italians who invented ice cream, although it did take until the 14th century. It is unlikely that he ever had a Yorkie, either. Nor did Catherine de Medici, who was known to be fond of a bowlful of Ben & Jerry's. It all started in Bradwell, although 366 years after Catherine started to put on weight. In 1899, Grandma Hannah Bradwell began to get ice sent by train from nearby Sheffield, which, given the steel industry, is about the last place on the planet you would have thought of as a supplier of cold things.

In her little cottage on Bridge Street, which is still a Bradwell's shop, she strutted her wonderful stuff, doing so by hand because she didn't have electricity. She developed many of the flavours that we know today, although more recently new flavours have become available, such as mango, which would have been unknown to Grandma Hannah, chocaccino, lemon curd and panna cotta, which is still unknown to 99% of the populace. (It is an infusion of cream, milk, sugar and gelatin, and was no doubt a favourite of Septimus Severus.)

The company was still in the hands of the Bradwell family until 1992, when it was bought by one Lawrence Wosskow, which is not a traditional Roman or Bradwell name. However, notwithstanding panna cotta, someone somewhere is doing a sterling job, and Bradwell's are still going strong. If the management of Bradwell's wish to acknowledge this tribute, they may send a huge consignment to the publishers of this volume, at the address inside the front cover. Double chocolate with hazelnut, please.

Bonsall Hen Racing

First chicken over the line is the winner, although, since the chickens don't know that, they aren't particularly bothered, so nearest to the line wins.

YOU could be forgiven for getting the wrong impression about Bonsall. You wouldn't be the first, and you probably won't be the last. To some, it is a sleepy village, with a former pub called the Pig of Lead, which gives you an idea of what industry the village was built on. To others, it is the very epicentre of UFO-spotting in England.

One rather hopes that UFO-spotting is not like the same thing with trains, whereby you must have an anorak and a notebook, and stand on the end of a platform somewhere exciting like Birmingham New Street, getting damp and writing down disparate numbers, with only a Thermos of tea for warmth.

However, between October 2000 and October 2002, there were 19 UFO sightings. This may be due in part to the two excellent hostelries in the village, the Barley Mow and the Kings Head, because it is hard to imagine that if little green men with antennae were to land on earth that they could choose somewhere as remote as Bonsall. You would think that either they wanted to come down in secrecy, where they would never be noticed, or would want to make as big an impact as possible.

If you had navigated your way to Derbyshire all the way from Betelgeuse, you would doubtless want to show off a bit, which would probably mean landing in Chesterfield, at the very least. Not that anybody would take a lot of notice, we've all got busy lives to get on with, but there's a sight more to look at, all things considered. Of course, it may well be that parking for flying saucers is at a premium in Chesterfield, you'd have to ask a Traffic Warden.

On the other hand, the men from Mars might be on a cultural search, and have heard about the goings-on in Bonsall, for it is the home of hen racing. The tradition died out for quite a while, but was brought alive again in 1991 by the landlord of the Barley Mow, who was fed up with gazing into the heavens looking for the 11.27 from the Horsehead Nebula.

It goes without saying, which usually means that somebody is going to say it, and today is no exception, that this is an opportunity for loads of fowl jokes, but I decided to chicken out, since not only are such things somewhat poultry, but one might finish up before the beak.

Anyway, what do you need to know about hen racing? Quite simply, the competitors

The men from Mars might be on a cultural search, and have heard about the goings-on in Bonsall

are placed on a track, and, with the crowd deadly quiet so as not to disturb them, race toward a finishing line 65ft away. Well, some of them do, anyway. Others go off in any direction, wander around in ever-decreasing circles, or merely show off their plumage to all and sundry. First chicken over the line is the winner, although, since the chickens don't know that, they aren't particularly bothered, so nearest to the line wins.

Candidly, it would save sports such as golf so much time and effort if they played "nearest the hole" rather than this overly pedantic business of getting the ball actually in the hole. There have been some great competitors over the years - chickens, I mean, not golfers - although sadly those from medieval times are unrecorded.

Presumably, literacy wasn't a pre-requisite for living in Bonsall, any more than the likelihood of the average ealdorman, sharing a pint of mead with a couple of aethelings, a thegn or two and the odd vassal and serf, looking to the skies, and asking: "How dost thou spell UFO?"

Today's chickens, though, have great names, noble names, names with gravitas, such as Snoopy, Nibor the Terrible, Bismark, Obama, Drumsticks, Eggletina and, of course, Half Beak. Mock at your peril.

Brailsford Ploughing Match

All you have to do is latch the plough on the back, tootle over to the field, lower the kit and drive up and down for a bit.

ASK today's city child where the peas on his plate came from, and the odds are he will say Tesco, or whichever supermarket his mum uses. He is, as all children, entirely right, but would only be so in the eyes of a lawyer, who tend to think in the simplest of terms, whilst using the most complex of terms, and charging you the earth for the privilege.

There is doubtless a Latin phrase for this, but, as you would expect, Adhuc sub judice lis est. However, the peas (this holds good for other vegetables, except Swedes, which are the work of Beelzebub) did not get to Tesco without some help, and this from a man in a flat cap.

We have advanced a long way, what with technology that can bake spuds in seconds, and make aeroplanes go faster than a bullet, which is why so many supersonic military aircraft nearly shoot themselves down. But the technology of the pea has not changed a deal, all things considered.

It is common nowadays to smother the crop with expensive chemicals, to keep off the gremlins, or the blight, and to aid growth, much like those cruel parents who give their kids cod-liver oil.

Today there is an alternative, known as Organics. This is relatively simple. As anyone who keeps animals knows, after feeding them, there is an inevitable by-product. If you have a small number of horses, for the sake of argument, this by-product is very good for the roses. If, on the other hand, you happen to have a few hundred head of Herefords, say, or Friesians, the by-product is produced in industrial quantities, and is not really the thing you want lying about the place. It attracts flies.

What you therefore do, since this stuff is free, cows never having been known to charge for it, (although bulls quite possibly might charge), is give it to those who have crops, who will find a use for it.

You, being smarter than the average cow, may well charge a small amount, perhaps for transportation, since it is not the kind of thing you would want to take in polythene bags on the bus. However, no matter how much you charge, the by-product is still produced, and must be got rid of. This relationship between the farmer of cattle and the farmer of crops is an extremely convenient one, and is known in professional circles as "Dead Handy".

Of one thing you can be certain; this stuff, whilst no doubt a shade niffy, is a sight less pricy than 2,4-dichlorophenoxyacetic acid or methyl isocyanate, which most cows know very little about, and therefore it is cheaper to use the brown stuff. That is why organic foods cost more in the supermarkets.

The man in the flat cap, however, as well as being an expert on all forms of fertilisation (although he may use slightly different terminology in one or two cases), knows what is best for his peas/carrots/Maris Pipers/leeks. He also knows that in order to plant the little thingies that make the vegetable jump up out of the ground, it is necessary to make a hole deep enough for them to stay warm in during the winter. Stop me if this is getting too technical for you.

Now, you could just go out in to the Vorty Acre Vield with a spade, dig a hole, and bung the thingies in, but this takes ages, and you'll never remember where you put them. Well, not without millions of those little flags such as archaeologists use, and that would cost a fortune. With the sheer physical effort, you would find yourself flagging by dinner time.

Instead, there is a simpler, quicker and more cost effective way, once you've forked out a mere £29,750 on a used tractor, and a further £600-or-so on a plough. Nobody said that farming was easy. All you have to do is latch the plough on the back, tootle over to the field, lower the kit and drive up and down for a bit. Well, that's what they make it look like, but don't be fooled, not for one teeny weeny little minute. Ploughing is a major art, to the extent that there is even a Society of Ploughmen, and if you want to find out just how complicated it can get, take a shufti at their website.

One thing that the Society of Ploughmen does is to regulate all the Ploughing Matches in the country. A Ploughing Match is just that, where men who make a living from the soil showcase their skills, trying to produce the perfect furrow.

Most of us wouldn't know what the perfect furrow looks like. Apparently it's all to do with the way you set the mouldboard up, and making sure that the point at the front of the diggy-bit isn't too sharp. And a hundred other things, added to which you've got to be able to drive your tractor in a straight line. Just try driving one in a straight line on a Tarmac surface, and you will start to see how monstrously difficult it can be over a field. Just one word of advice - don't use Tarmac roads in South Yorkshire, they tend to be more rutted than the average ploughed field to start with.

The Ploughing Match at Brailsford, which is more properly a Ploughing and Hedge-Cutting Match, has been going for well over 100 years, and looks like it will keep going for as long as peas and carrots are with us. Sadly, it has had to be cancelled in some years for things like Foot and Mouth Disease, but the farming community isn't easy to rattle, and they carry on as soon as they can.

The Match is not just for modern tractors, but vintage ones as well, and even for horse-drawn ploughs. There are hedging competitions, using techniques that might look old-fashioned, but that are still the most effective. After all, the hedge hasn't changed much over the years, it's just that we see fewer of them than of yore. Other competitions include walking-stick making, which is a fine form of artistry.

The next time you walk into a pub called The Plough, or even if you look up at the constellation that the purist would call Ursa Major, spare a thought for those experts, who not only display great skills at their trade, but also keep the freezers full at Sainsbury's.

Castleton Garland

Oak Apple Day is celebrated every year, by the simple expedient of covering a man with a whole pyramid of flowers, then putting him on a horse so that he can't see a thing.

IF, like thousands of others in this sceptred isle, you suffer from any allergies, May 29th is not a good day for you. It is the sort of day when you would be best advised to take a day off work, stay in bed with an inhaler and a packet of tablets and feel sorry for yourself.

Hayfever is one of those unpleasant afflictions that those who have never had it refer to it as "a touch of hayfever", whilst the sufferer has a nose that does a fair impression of Niagara Falls, eyes full of grit, a throat full of razor blades and starts to lose the will to live after a few weeks of misery, knowing that the end to it will not come until there is another "r" in the month. Of course, all the aforegoing is irrelevant if you are a fireman, and especially in Derbyshire. For 29th May is Oak Apple Day, and no more so is it than in Castleton.

This is the day, each year, when the good and honest burghers of the village dress up in strange clothes, get the horses out of the stable, and prepare to visit every pub in the vicinity. It is strange how so many of the county's customs seem to involve the consumption of vast amounts of alcohol, although this is to be applauded.

However, at this point, you are asking yourself what oak apples have got to do with hayfever, and a very good question it is, too, especially if you are reading this with half-a-pound of Vaseline up your conk, and a box of tissues on your lap. The answer is, nothing. Well, not very much, anyway.

Oak Apple Day is celebrated in downtown Castleton every year, by the simple expedient of covering a man with a whole pyramid of flowers, that reach down to below his waist, then they put him on a horse, so that he can't see a thing. This man is King for the day. He also has a Queen, as you would expect, although whether she bears the role of an helpmeet, as Eve did for Adam, is a moot point. You'd have to be royalty to find out.

Anyway, the Queen too is on horseback, and the pair of them parade through every street, along with the local band and hordes of young girls dressed in white. The planners of this spectacle are obviously the wise men of the community, for there are various ports of call, these being The Castle, The George, The Bull's Head, The Peak, Ye Olde Nags Head and Ye Olde Cheshire Cheese.

Whilst the King and Queen must perforce stay dry, droit de siegneur and all that, never mind the old dignity bit, playing the cornet is thirsty work, and liquid sustenance is necessary. It is equally thirsty work playing the euphonium, the trombone or the triangle.

That little stick thing is heavy, it's made of metal, and there's all that counting of beats to do. It's even worse for the drummers, so a swift libation in each of the aforementioned hostelries is abshlutly eshenshl.

Of course, by the time that the procession reaches the final haven of light and presumably bitter, the music is at best avant garde. The majority may well be playing Men of Harlech, but there is no reason why the kettle drummer shouldn't sing Nellie Dean if he so wishes, and therefore he usually does.

The King, Queen and various others are dressed in Stuart clothing, which is, whilst fascinating, slightly misleading. It seems that May 29th was the birthday of Charles II, to whom fell the fall of the foul fiend Cromwell and the Restoration of the Monarchy, and was pronounced as being a holiday and "to be for ever kept as a day of thanksgiving for our redemption from tyranny and the King's return to his government, he entering London on that day."

True to their word, most of England kept that "for ever" until 1859, a singularly short eternity, but Castleton is not to be defeated or cowed. Some would claim that the date is to commemorate the Battle of Worcester, which was held very close to May 29th, on 3rd September 1651, and which the King lost anyway. Actually, Charles II was so peeved with Mr Cromwell that his remains were dug up and his head chopped off, which must have been a fun day for the coroner, especially since the dear departed had shuffled off this mortal coil some two years previously, in 1658.

So popular was the Lord Protector that his severed head was carted by various mendicant ghouls around the kingdom, prior to being auctioned off in 1814. The auctioneer's catalogue would have made interesting reading. The head was eventually buried, on 25th March 1960, at his old college, Sidney Sussex, Cambridge. You have to hope it had been left in the care of the headmaster.

It is unlikely, however, that the Oak Apple Day, or Garland Day celebrations, are originally from the 18th century. Whilst there is a certain pleasing symmetry about Charles II hiding in an oak tree, and thus taking the oak apple for his symbol, it seems far more likely that it is an ancient fertility rite, although what a chap is supposed to do with half the village looking on, and with a hundredweight of flowers covering him is anybody's guess.

Certainly, oak leaves are handed out, which have long been held to be a symbol of fertility, although greenfly can be a bit of a dampener. Not that Charles II was short in the fertility stakes, having had at least 12 illegitimate children from a minimum of six mistresses, ranging from Barbara Palmer (officially named Lady of the Bedchamber, although what Charles' wife, Catherine of Braganza, thought is not for these genteel pages,) to dear old Nell Gwynne. No wonder they called him the Merrie Monarche, and similarly, little wonder that nowadays they keep him under a huge pyramid of flowers, to keep him out of harm's way.

Of course, nobody expects the poor old monarch to keep his crown of flora on for the rest of the day, especially since he must be acutely aware of his loyal subjects pouring vast quantities of liquified hops down their throats, and playing notes that Mozart would never have recognised. Eventually, the procession finds its way to the local church and the crown and King are separated, the former being hoisted up to the top of the tower, there to wither.

The church, incidentally, is dedicated to St Edmund, who was King of the East Angles, and a fairly bloodthirsty cove to boot, which is always a boon to the unsuspecting saint. He died in 869 AD, and was buried at, would you believe, Bury St Edmunds, which is rather convenient for the chronicler of history. How he would have felt about another king, albeit a floral one, deposing him is not on record, and nor do we know what he would have had to say about pagan rites in his church, although one rather gets the feeling that heads would have rolled, once they had emerged from their petally hiding-place.

What would have happened if St Edmund had suffered from hayfever, or, worse yet, an allergy to horses, can only be imagined. The devout will doubtless light a candle to him, but this is not advisable. There is enough risk of fire as it is, without adding to the problem, especially with all those dried up flowers hanging about. How so? Linear history is very simple.

If Charles II were alive today, not only would Nell be getting a bit wrinkly and her oranges looking a bit less than juicy, but there would be 379 candles on his birthday cake. No wonder the poor old Derbyshire firemen can't take the day off on May 29th.

Chapel-en-le-Frith Curfew Bell

Just at the moment when this book slips from your fingers to land with a gentle "plop" on the Axminster, the whole room will shake with the sound of bells.

THE Bells! The Bells! It was the Bells that made me deaf, Esmarelda." You, of course, being erudite and well-read will not for one moment think that Victor Hugo was referring to the brand of Scotch Whisky, since it has little effect on the hearing. The memory, yes, but not the hearing.

Now, where were we? Oh, yes, Quasimodo. As we all know, he was the bell-ringer of Notre Dame Cathedral, at which point you start wondering what has all this got to do with Derbyshire. Is there going to be some strange conspiracy theory whereby Hugo came from Swadlincote, or Quasimodo himself was not an orphan, but had trained originally in Holmesfield? Not so. Esmeralda, by the way, was a beautiful 16-year-old gypsy dancer who had never been anywhere near Ault Hucknall, despite one or two rumours heard in the bar of Glapwell Miners Welfare.

However, the sound of bells is not unknown in the county. Of course not, you think, there are church bells before services, there are chiming clocks that bong across the landscape, frightening crows and dislodging slates, there are those merry peals when some wedding is soon to take place, or those where a more solemn occasion is about to begin.

Not as bad as the custom in the village of Sasbach am Kaiserstuhl, in southern Germany. There, when somebody dies, a peal is rung, followed by another half-an-hour later, and another a further half-hour on. Then, a bell is tolled for every year of the deceased's age. I only heard this once, and realised that there is no linguistic equivalent for "ninety-four - that's a good long innings!" least of all at four in the morning with the bell tower a scant 40 feet from one's head.

Sasbach, however, does not mind if (provided you are not deceased) you stay up late, so long as you do not make any unnecessary noise. The village pub, called the White Lion, or Die Weisse Loewe if you prefer, shuts when the last customer leaves, and a very civilised arrangement it is too.

The local councils around Baden-Wurttemberg are a fairly liberal crowd, which cannot, sadly, be said for those in Chapel-en-le-Frith. Maybe it is something to do with the Norman heritage, hence the rather French-sounding name, meaning the Chapel in the Forest Clearing. This was at one time a hunting lodge for the Norman Nobs. You often get the feeling that they were a fairly strait-laced lot, what with Domesday Books and the like.

In the year 1070, the Norman aristocracy decided that a curfew bell should be rung, to keep the peasants out of mischief. The churches didn't want to spend too

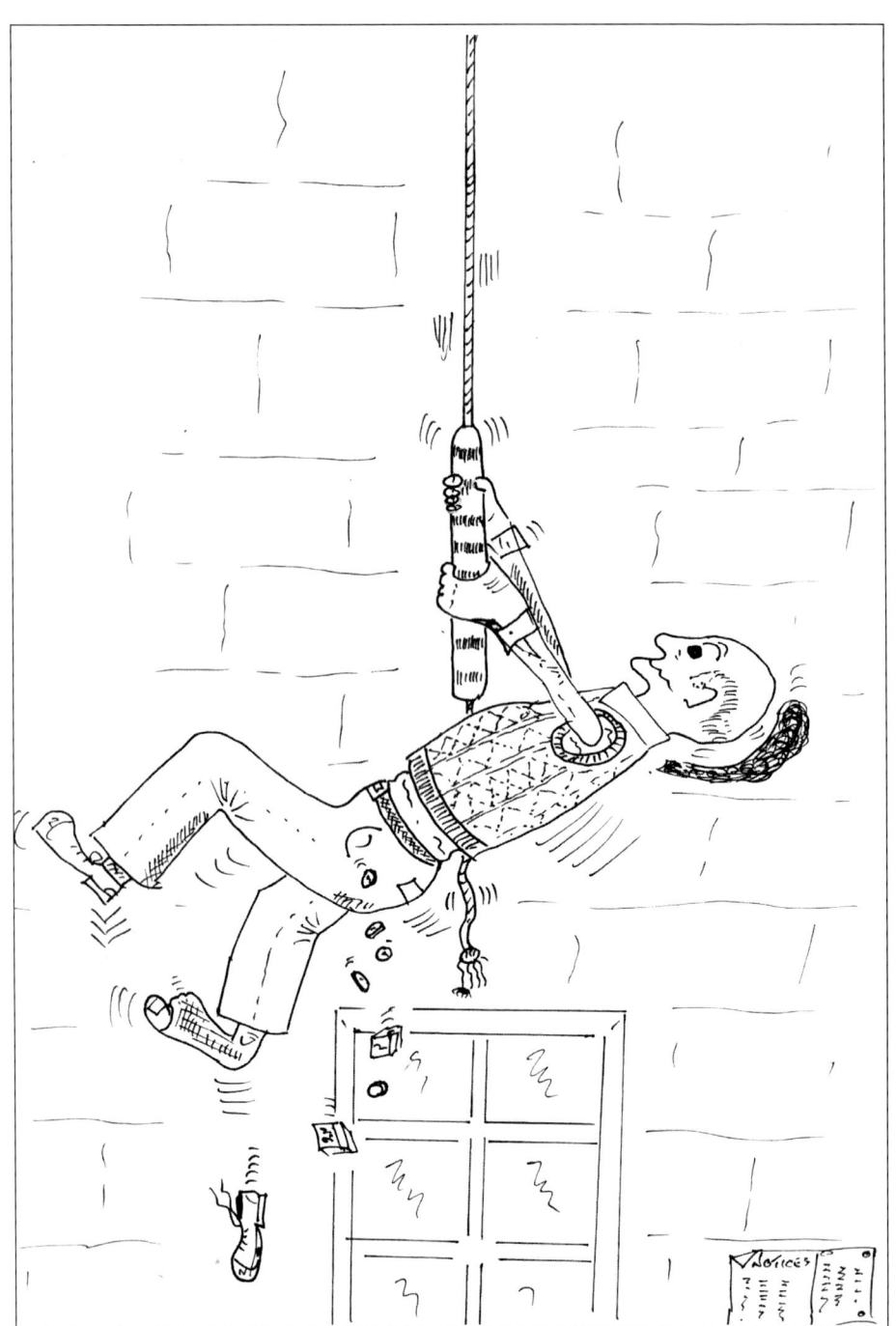

Chapel is one of several places in Derbyshire that encourage its inhabitants to retire to their little truckle beds earlier than Channel 5 would like you to

much time listening to confessions, it gets a bit tedious, and if you keep the troops locked up, there is less risk.

By one of those strange quirks of fate, the Curfew Bell is still rung in Chapel-en-le-Frith, which seems a bit odd. One of the main reasons was to let the hoi-polloi know that it was time to damp the fire down for the night, yet Chapel is now a smokeless zone, with many a radiator to the fore.

Secondly, if you think what rubbish the denizens of Goggle-Box House bung at us after the nine o'clock watershed, when all the little kiddies have gone up the wooden hill to Bedfordshire, there is probably more scope for a touch of immorality inside your own home than down the boozer, with the neighbours watching your every move.

Presumably, nowadays you are exempt from getting belted round the back of the nut with a knobkerrie and being dragged off down the local nick for the night, followed by porridge and off to court on the morrow.

So, you deduce, Chapel is possibly not the place to live, but how wrong you would be. Not only is it a very nice town, and close to the canal basin at Whaley Bridge, it is one of several places in Derbyshire that encourage its inhabitants to retire to their little truckle beds earlier than Channel 5 would like you to. Obviously, they do not go along with the old saw of "Early to bed, early to rise, makes a man healthy, wealthy and wise." The person who told me that one was a coughing wreck who was flat broke because he was unwise enough to blow all his coins on fags and booze.

So, where else are the nightbirds discouraged? Well, it still happens in Winster, at eight in the evening (before the watershed) and Castleton at seven. Here the medium tone bell, Number Five, is rung for approximately eight minutes, then the Number Seven bell is rung with the day's date - which, if it is the thirty-first, must be hard work. The poor old bell-ringer doesn't get too fatigued, though, because it only happens on a Saturday.

Ashford has a curfew bell, as does Dronfield, although, rather conveniently, right opposite the church is the Green Dragon, so it is possible to get a mental image of someone scuttling across the road, ringing his bell for a bit, then nipping back to finish his pint.

Sadly, the practice has now discontinued in Chesterfield, but at one stage it was used to call the French prisoners of war, who were allowed out during the day, back to their huts and a bit of the old couchez.

Finally, the church at Scarcliffe still sounds the curfew, but only for three weeks either side of Christmas. This is still funded the way it was eight hundred years ago, by means of the Bellrope Charity.

Of course, if you are on holiday as you are reading this, after a hard day's trekking around looking at things, and you fancy a bit of a nap before sliding out for a traditional glass of something with foam on the top, there is a downside. Just as you close your eyes, and that lovely feeling of peace and tranquillity overcomes you, just at the moment when this book slips from your fingers to land with a gentle "plop" on the Axminster, the whole room will shake with the sound of bells and you will be hurled back violently in to wakefulness. Do not worry. It's only the bell telling you that it is time to sleep.

Chesterfield Crooked Spire

It was built in 1362, when the Black Death was racing through the continent, which had two consequences, at least for Chesterfield's spire.

THEY knew how to name diseases, then. There were some great names, such as gaol fever, which has a far better ring to it than mere typhus. You could get ague, or maybe yellow fever, whilst the bloody flux, aka dysentery, was popular, at least in one sense of the word.

Indeed, if you were a poet, it was considered mandatory to die of consumption and if you could do it whilst somewhere exotic, such as Byron snuffing it in Messolonghi, you were quids in.

But there was a catch, as it were. You could not get a bit of something - you had to do the job properly. You didn't get "a touch of the scorbutics", you got scurvy, and unless someone was a bit quick with the vitamin C you were, especially if you were in the Royal Navy, going to get entered in the Ship's Log as 'Discharged Dead'.

But the grandaddy of them all, the Big One so to speak was the Black Death. The name alone tells you all you need to know. It was sufficiently virulent that you might well wake up on Monday feeling a bit rough and by Tuesday they were putting your name in the 'Deaths' column of the parish register.

We only have to be grateful that there were no tabloid newspapers in those days - they caused enough panic with Asian flu, Spanish flu, Bird flu, Hong-Kong flu, Swine flu and presumably One Flew over the Cuckoo's nest. The only disease about which the redtops have not caused alarm and despondency is Alice. This is because they don't know what it is, exactly, only that Christopher Robin went down with it.

So what has all this medical meandering got to do with us? Because, were it not for the Black Death, most people would probably never have heard of Chesterfield. It would have gone down in history as sharing a name with an over-stuffed type of settee.

Yet, and it seems a curiously symbiotic relationship, because of the Black Death Chesterfield is famous, if only for the spire of its church. As everybody knows, it is considerably out of true, to the tune of nine feet six inches, or 2.89 metres, whatever they are. Close to a yard, I seem to recall.

The spire was built in 1362, when the Black Death was racing through the continent, which had two consequences, at least for Chesterfield's spire. Firstly, a lack of skilled workmen led to unseasoned wood being used, it being easier to work with for the non-expert, and secondly, the standard of workmanship was not as good as it would have been just a couple of decades earlier.

As a result it leans quite dramatically to the south west. However, the twist in the spire, at least according to some experts, is sufficiently regular that it was in all probability deliberate. Unfortunately, we will never know.

There is yet another theory that people were so a-feared of catching the Plague that they developed an 'Eat, Drink, for Tomorrow we Die' attitude, and spent a bit longer than is advisable in the local taverns, instead of getting the plumb-bob to the spire. Frankly, that seems a bit less than plausible, if colourful.

They had the same problem in Barnstaple, at about the same time, and presumably for much the same reasons. The third crooked spire in Britain is at Cleobury Mortimer, in Shropshire, but they're having none of this nonsense; theirs is due to damp-induced rot, which is not half so romantic.

There is a certain something that supports the excessive booze theory, though, in that whilst we have only three crooked spires, France, a country noted for its predilection for the grape, has more than 65. Of course, it may be that they just had rubbish architects. Germany (Bier and Schnapps) has 22, but dour Switzerland (Toblerone) has a mere four. The other side of the coin is that Italy (Chianti) has only the one. Make of this what you will.

Incidentally, the lead sheets on the Chesterfield spire weigh in at an impressive 32 tons, and it is only that weight which stops the spire blowing off in a stiff breeze. Mind you, it would have to be extremely stiff, given that it is circular in section, and anyway, it has been there for more than 650 years without a problem, so, whilst Health and Safety are no doubt having kittens as they read this, and looking out the Bostik, there is nothing to worry about.

All that having been said, you can't just have a simple bit of reasoning like that, because it is far too mundane for words - or for tourists, come to that. You need something with a bit more panache, a bit more life, a bit more pzazz. Strangely, the main legend concerning Chesterfield, for we shall leave those sur le Continong to sort it out for themselves, centres around the Devil.

Bear in mind that his name, Satan, means "slanderer" or "liar", so you will not be surprised to know that what follows is either slanderous or a pack of lies. Of course, some of it is merely slanderous lies, or lying slander, but it is entertaining nonetheless.

Legend one says that a young lady entered the church to be married, and she was so beautiful that the spire bent down to get a better look. This implies that the remainder of the young ladies of the borough, since the fourteenth century, have wavered between being plain and being not unlike the north end of a southbound yak. This is slanderous.

Alternatively, the same young lady turned up for her wedding, and the devil, sitting atop the spire was so surprised that she was - how to put this delicately? - virgo intacta, that he fell, only preventing himself from hitting the deck some 228 feet below by wrapping his tail around the spire, pulling it out of true.

Since other legends, no more believable, say that Satan is an accomplished aeronaut, with his own wings, this theory is both slanderous and a lie. There is even a corollary to this, yet more slanderous, which says that the next time a bride who has remained, shall we say, unsullied, turns up, the spire will right itself. Hmmm. Just as a snippet to fill up a tiny corner of your prodigious memory, flying is defined as the art of throwing yourself at the ground, and missing.

Again, the devil was sitting atop the spire during a service. (It rather makes one wonder why he had such a fascination with Chesterfield, Sheffield isn't that far away as the fallen angel flies). It was a singularly High Church service, complete with incense, which made him sneeze - well, it would - and again, he fell.

Alternatively, after which you may put your credulity back to wherever you normally keep it, a magician forced a Bolsover blacksmith to shoe the devil, but the blacksmith was either incompetent, a sadist, or a devout churchman, for the nail was driven into the devil's foot, causing him to fly away in a rage, and when, in a fit of satanic pique, he lashed out with the injured foot, he caught the spire. Not necessarily slanderous, merely slightly less than truthful.

So, in conclusion, there's not much you can say about the legends surrounding the crooked spire in Chesterfield really, except that they are, as you would expect, devilishly interesting.

There is a theory that people were so a-feared of catching the Plague that they spent a bit longer than is advisable in the local taverns

Chesterfield Market

There is documentary evidence that there was a 'new' market in the town in 1165, and you can't have a new market without having an old one to replace.

WE can be pretty sure that Baldwin IX, Count of Flanders, never visited Chesterfield Market. Whilst the market was being granted its charter in 1204, Baldwin was a bit busy, if only being crowned First Emperor of the Latin Empire.

Obviously, he'd have had a lot to do; there's all those parties, and when you get to be Top Banana there are hordes of people tramping to your door, with ideas about this, that and the other. Then, there's time nipping down to the jewellers to have the crown re-sized, they never look quite right on the first day, and you'd have to have your suit of armour changed - it wouldn't do to turn up for your first battle in a kit that made it look like you were a mere count, it wouldn't give the troops any confidence at all.

The interior decorators are going to be round, you wouldn't want to rule from a second-hand castle, and there would be loads of putting your mark on various bits of parchment. If you were really serious about being emperor, you'd have the local graphologist round of a Tuesday night for a week or so, teaching you how to sign your name.

You just wouldn't be able to hold your head up in public ever again, if everybody around you put a flowing signature on the bottom of the latest treaty and all you could manage was a shaky 'X'.

Of course, it was all in vain, because the following year, Baldwin snuffed it, possibly with the aid of a gentleman carrying a sharp instrument, and Tsar Kaloyan reputedly had his skull made into a drinking vessel. It is unsure whether this is true, since the phrase "just nipping out for a cranium" has never passed into any language.

King John was a dab hand at signatures. There are those that say he was illiterate, which is why he put his seal on the Magna Carta, but it ain't necessarily so. It was customary for all parties to append their seal, but it doesn't mean that His Majesty couldn't read or write, because he could.

Anyway, if he signed the Royal Charter granting Chesterfield a market, it may well have been practice for the Magna Carta, which was 15 years down the line. It was also very good of him, because this was during the Crusades and the gallant lads, slaughtering all and sundry in the name of the Prince of Peace, had just taken Constantinople, so he may well have had other things to do. You can't run a Crusade without paperwork, you know.

This means that Chesterfield has had a market, consistently, for more than 800 years, and against all the odds. More than one market, actually. King John liked the idea of multiple markets, so there are things happening on Mondays, Fridays and Saturdays, plus a farmers' market on the second Thursday and the last Sunday of the month. There is a fish market where you can buy fish, a meat market for your meat requirements, a clothes market for getting clothes at, and a flea market....

But, there's more. There is documentary evidence that there was a 'new' market in the town in 1165, and you can't have a new market without having an old one to replace it with. Indeed, to prove that it existed, it coughed up £1/2/7d to the Sheriff of Derbyshire. So, it doesn't matter how you look at it, there has been a market around for what is known in historical circles as "Donkey's Years". And if that isn't a tradition, then what is?

There has been a market around in Chesterfield for what is known in historical circles as "Donkey's Years"

Coal Aston Hook and Hoop

It is said that the game is used by the young bloods to gain standing within the community, although nobody openly admits the fact. Well, be fair, would you?

YOU wouldn't want to argue with a bull. They tend to be a bit on the large side and not necessarily noted for their sweetness of temper. This is perhaps one reason why there used to be such barbaric sports as bull-baiting, whereby the bull was tethered to a ring, sometimes had pepper blown up its nose, to make it even more bad tempered, and then it was set upon by dogs.

Strange to relate, it was a form of entertainment, although when you think about it, it's no worse than bull-fighting, which flourishes in some parts of the world. It's no better, either, which fact was eventually realised in 1835, although the Bill took 33 years to get through Parliament (draw your own conclusion) and mercifully it was banned.

There are still vestiges of this nasty practice left, though, for example in the name of that well-known shopping centre in Birmingham. Mind you, there is also something for the argument that wandering around indoor shopping malls, fighting your way through crowds, being trodden on, having your nostrils assailed by the continual smell of fast foods, getting your pocket picked and then not being able to find your car afterwards, never mind paying prices double of those in the local market, is pretty barbaric as well, but now is not the right time for that.

Incidentally, there is also a Bull Ring, the actual metal ring to which the poor animal was tied, in Eyam. For those of a curious nature, it is on the left just as you get in to the village, outside the baker's shop. It will come as no shock to find out that there was, as ever, an "excuse" for this barbaric behaviour, as some kind souls maintained that it made the meat more tender. Similar hollow-sounding excuses have been used for other blood sports for many a long year.

In order for farmers to be able to move the bull from place to place, given that it was unlikely to respond to sweet reason, when still young it had a ring put through the end of its nose, which is no worse, apparently, than having your ears pierced. I wouldn't know. The ring is still seen today, not only on bulls, although you are advised not to look too closely - despite their girth, they are notoriously sensitive animals - but also in pubs. This is the point at which the boggle enters the mind.

There is a pub game called Ringing the Bull, which is practised in only a handful of pubs throughout the queendom. Not surprisingly (or it wouldn't be in this book), there is a pub in Derbyshire where this ancient game continues. However, unlike the Trip to Jerusalem in

Nottingham, say, where 'tis boasted that they play the game as the Crusaders did, Derbyshire has put its own stamp upon things, but they call it Hook and Hoop. Not perhaps the most imaginative name you've ever heard, but it's good enough for the regulars at the Royal Oak, in Coal Aston. Not that the regulars would refer to going down to the Royal Oak for a pint, they would talk about The Pond, for that is this fine hostelry's traditional name.

Hook and Hoop is a game whereby a string, attached to the ceiling, has a ring on the end of it, customarily a bull's nose ring. On the wall is a hook, again, courtesy of the bull, since it was, at least at one time, a horn. The object, simply enough, is to swing the ring and get it to lodge over the hook. Easy. No it isn't, it is extremely difficult and takes a delicate touch, because if you get your level of force wrong, the ring either doesn't get there at all, or else it bounces off. Get the angle wrong, and you will miss the target to either side, and no doubt the greater the miss, the louder the hilarity.

It is said that the game is used by the young bloods to gain standing within the community, although nobody openly admits the fact. Well, be fair, would you? Added to which, it is better than bull or bear baiting, or, indeed, shopping malls.

There is a legend that a young lady in the village stated that the men gained no kudos whatsoever, and that as a punishment she was tied to the hoop for a total of four days, four hours, four minutes and four seconds, this being Ye Ancient Tradition. Is it true? Well, it could be, but on the other hand, it could be a load of old bull.

Cresswell Crags Artwork

History suggests that the caves were occupied during the Ice Age, which others say is impossible, because there was a one-and-a-half-mile thick sheet of ice over the country.

FEW things can be more irritating than waking up one morning, wandering your way to the bus stop as usual and finding that some mindless poltroon has sneaked up in the night and made what he considers to be improvements.

When you got home last night, you were not aware that some clown who has invented a squiggly way of writing something meaningless even existed, but now, it seems like the whole area is covered in the fruits of his aerosol labours. Worse yet, instead of just calling it criminal damage, some Flash Harry with an eye for the main chance decided to dub it Graffiti, and imbue it with an air of respectability.

What can be done about this modern phenomenon? Actually, listen to the vast majority of radio phone-ins, of which there are a plethora in Derbyshire, and the most appropriate punishment would seem to range from public flogging through the re-introduction of the stocks, to the ever-popular hanging. This is known as "Trial by Dimwit".

The first and most obvious question is, when did this anti-social practice rear its ugly head? Aha, you say, for that is what people are wont to say when they have come up with a solution, including the building of a gallows, just in case. There are, somebody points out, incidents of graffiti in ancient Pompeii, including a rather scurrilous cartoon of a politician on a public wall. The perpetrator of this dastardly crime was never hanged, for a dirty great cloud of poison gas whistling in at a couple of hundred miles an hour, in 79 AD, did the job far more efficiently. So, was the Roman Empire responsible for Graffiti? Not a cat's chance, although the word is partly their fault, etymology being the item that it is. But there are far older bits of wall-scribbling yet.

Go through the Derbyshire village of Cresswell, an old mining community, and just before you get in to Nottinghamshire, at the precise point when the slag-heap from England's most tragic mine hoves into view on your right-hand side, turn left, and drive down one of the narrowest roads you will come across, without it being called a cart track. At the bottom of the road, after a bit of meandering, you will find Cresswell Crags. Those people who lived there, many many years ago, and scuttled around the caves in animal skins, did not have to worry about the traffic lights on the way in - they were a slightly later addition.

History suggests, a phrase which means that nobody can agree, that the caves were occupied during the Ice Age, which others will say is impossible, because there was a one-and-a-half-mile thick sheet of ice over the country, which tends to blot out the sun.

44

Others say it was later, during that time in history when Britain was fumbling around with tools made from antlers and flint, and the Egyptians were just standing back and taking an admiring look at the pyramids. Whilst our forebears were throwing lumps of rock at marauding bears, the temple in Jerusalem was not just built, but being decorated with ornate carvings of gold, silver and copper. They were using precious stones, not just for the buildings, but for the clothing of the High Priest, who looked far better dressed than the average caveman, all things considered. They had a judicial system second to none, health regulations, in fact just about everything bar low-flush loos and street lights. Actually, if you wish to be really pedantic, there were regulations, quite clear and concise,

The cave artists of Cresswell were ordinary people, who, like the rest of us, wanted to make their homes look at least semi-reasonable

on the disposal of human waste, but we will go no further with that line of enquiry.

It is not our brief, you and I, to concern ourselves about exactly how old the cave art of Cresswell really is, because it probably doesn't matter much to we ordinary folk. It is a bit like worrying yourself into sleeplessness about whether the correct spelling is Bouddica or Boadicea, it won't alter the fact that she was prone to charging around slaughtering Romans before anybody else got round to hanging them for drawing things in places they shouldn't. All we need to know is that the artwork is very, very old and since some of the caves were known to have been inhabited as late as the Roman occupation of Britain, it's probably not worth letting it spoil your lunch.

Most of the art inside the caves is of animals, and, whilst not wishing to be critical of artists who had little in the way of modern aids, they are rudimentary. The best is of a large stag, with quite imposing antlers, and when you consider that even today Cresswell is right on the edge of Sherwood Forest, which has shrunk considerably over the years, this fits in perfectly with what we know about the area even from relatively modern times. There is also a rather impressive bison.

However, our problem lies, not with the art, which was, all things considered, created for exactly the same reason as us going in to town and buying a replica Canneletto or Hockney, but with the experts who look at it and cloud the issue. If a cave artist, whether you class his work as graffiti or merely the pre-historic equivalent of Dulux, draws bison, deer and other animals, then all well and good. When he indulges himself with a few birds, and why not, Vaughan Williams got away with "The Lark Ascending", why on earth, so to speak, would you start waffling on about them being, and I quote, "female anthropomorphs"? Why not call them "ornithological paraphenomena" instead? They are birds. You know the sort of thing: sparrows, starlings, robins, blackbirds (at which point some will start bleating on about religious symbolism in the Stone Age) and so forth.

Obviously the drawings are not going to be of incredible accuracy, because there was no way of photographing them. Kodak was still in its infancy and if the only method of bringing one down was to sling rocks at it, the odds of getting one that was in half decent nick were pretty remote.

The cave artists of Cresswell were ordinary people, who, like the rest of us, wanted to make their homes look at least semi-reasonable, and Ikea was a few years off yet, never mind that the nearest one was in Nottingham. They had limited materials at hand, and fairly limited knowledge. If the Ice Age was forming overhead, their brush-holding hand would have been shivering slightly.

Wouldn't it be nice if, instead of strange men in beards propounding strange theories, we just accepted that civilisation isn't quite as new as we thought, and nor was the apportioning of talent. All we can say is that Derbyshire has a tradition of art and skill that goes back further than anywhere else in Britain, and that's good enough for us. Broadcast the fact. Phone your friends and tell them. Write about it, preach it from the rooftops, compose a musical about it, translate it into Coptic, if you wish. Just don't scrawl it on a wall.

Derby & Bonnie Prince Charlie

There is a petrol station just south of Markeaton where they might have picked up a sandwich or two, perhaps a buffet pork pie.

IF you and your friends were referred to as "wild, unwashed, barbarous savages", you might just, and with good reason, feel a bit peeved. We are on fairly safe ground here, because the average wild, unwashed, barbarous savage tends not to read things like this, but manages with certain tabloid newspapers and "Savages Weekly", a publication which is famous for the knitting patterns.

However, the accusation has been made, and it must be answered. Admittedly, it was made some while ago but the hurt is not lessened. In fact, since the gauntlet hit the floor, so to speak, it may well have ruined the holiday season, because whoever made the statement did so on December 4th, 1745. It wouldn't have been half so irritating as getting seven bells knocked out of your savages at Culloden Moor on April 16th, 1746, though. It was not a good year to be Charles Edward Stuart, although you could take solace that all your chaps called you Bonnie Prince Charlie. They obviously weren't as blue as they were painted.

Bonnie Prince Charlie was on his way to London, to claim the throne, which seemed to be a fairly popular pastime during one period in our history. Since the M1 wasn't quite finished at that time, it was necessary to nip down the A52 from Ashbourne to Derby, which is not the best place to be in mid-December. If one is wearing a kilt, or at least the 18th century equivalent, a plaid, it could get a touch draughty around the nether regions.

Anyway, it seems highly likely that the lads stopped for a bar-snack at the Rose and Crown in Kings Langley, although it seems equally likely that it had another name at that time. If not, it would have become known as the Pile of Ashes at Kings Langley. The locals might well have taken the village sign down, since savages don't like to think that there might be opposition.

Alternatively, there is a petrol station just south of Markeaton, where they might have picked up a sandwich or two, perhaps a buffet pork pie, or even, who knows, a slice of haggis. An army marches on its stomach, although there is many a footsore infantryman who might take issue with that remark, particularly outside Ashbourne in December.

Regrettably, if you are a Scot, they were going back north just two days later, with their collective tail between their legs. Despite the fact that news had travelled ahead that Charlie had nine or ten thousand men, over-egging the pudding somewhat, when he left

Since the M1 wasn't quite finished at that time, it was necessary for Bonnie Prince Charlie to nip down the A52 from Ashbourne to Derby

Ashbourne and its cheering crowds, he still expected a bit of a punch-up in Derby. The newly-formed Derby Blues, under the command of the Duke of Devonshire, contemplated their sworn role to safeguard the city in the event of savages, ummed and ahhed for a few minutes, and legged it bravely to Retford.

The Scots Army arrived in Derby, with fanfarade, bunting and frolics, and on reaching the George Inn asked for lodging for the night. There might have been a few beds, including that so very recently vacated by the heroic Duke, but it was a bit much asking for beds for 9,000 blokes, particularly as they hadn't booked. Anyway, a scant two days later, the Prince's advisors decided that since Government troops were on their way, in number, that now was the time to disappear back north, and stand not upon the order of their going.

The Prince, one assumes, was a lot less than happy, but did as he was bidden, after much chuntering about advisors, which, to this day, is a political tradition. The Army did as they were told, as armies do, although doubtless with a great deal of mumbling when the Sergeant Major couldn't hear. Fortunately, so incomprehensible were their accents, that the exact words couldn't be understood, and there is thus no need to offend the delicate sensibilities of a refined readership.

And so ended the Prince's pretensions, and, as it happens, his run of success. A scant four months later, his poor, tired army were beaten solidly at Culloden Moor, and the Prince escaped to France, in to exile, there to die an alcoholic. This is a tradition in France. Happily for us, the Prince is not forgotten in England today.

In the Yere of Grace MCMXCV did ye goodlie sculptor Anthony Stones, his statue in ye Citie of Derbye unveil, to whit Ye Prince Charles Edward Stuart, aboard his trusty steed, which sadly remains nameless. It is a brilliant statue, by any standard. Each year since then, the Charles Edward Stuart Society have held a pageant to commemorate Bonnie Prince Charlie's visit, if such a mundane word is adequate, to the city.

It is so well thought of, that members of the Royal Stuart Society attend, when battles are re-enacted, albeit perhaps rather more enthusiastically than the original, and a wreath laid at the foot of the statue. It is to commemorate an event that history attests to, although not to the fantastic legends, such as the Prince fathering a child on the visit.

One suspects his mind might have been on other things, with 9,000 savages wandering around outside the bedroom window. He is also accredited with staying at any number of places, which means he must have had a pretty disturbed night, one way and the other.

It is interesting to speculate what might have happened if the Bonnie Prince had reached London and got his father back on the throne. Our whole history would be entirely different, although we would still have the skirl of the pipes at Balmoral on a regular basis, and maybe Scotch Whisky wouldn't be so heavily taxed. Just in case the Young Pretenders claims are proved, in later years, it might be worth remembering that whisky can be Scotch, as can beef, broth, tape, egg, fir, etc, etc - but everything else is Scottish.

And don't mention "savages". You have been warned!

Derby Florentine Boar

The good people of Derby have come over all Italian, and taken to patting the nose of the boar, as they go past it.

IT is an honour, nay, a privilege, to report on a new tradition, if that is not an oxymoron. Actually, it is not a new tradition at all, at least, not if you live in Florence, because you would have been doing this since about 1612.

That is what people in Florence did. In fact, they did it so much, that a new nose was ordered in 1857, so it is still old enough to be traditional. Actually, that's not entirely true, it wasn't just a new nose, it was a whole boar. And even the 1612 one wasn't exactly new, it was a copy of one made a couple of centuries BC, by Greek or Greeks unknown.

The one in Florence was a bronze, cast by one Pietro Tacca, but it was a copy of the Greek one, which had been marble. This was in turn, eventually, copied by Mr William John Coffee of Derby, but bronze isn't cheap stuff, so it was made in terracotta. Derby, of course, has no shortage of the right clays for such things.

Of course, the good Mr Coffee didn't just make it on a whim, or if he did, it was on the whim of Joseph Strutt, son of Jedediah, a local textile manufacturer and philanthropist. Presumably, Mr Coffee was proud of his work, but we are no longer in a position to ask him, since he emigrated to New York in 1816, and he is not listed in the phone book.

However, proud he should be, for the grounds in which he built his boar are now the Arboretum in Derby, which is also the first public park in England, thus making his the first public boar in England. A man can be proud of such achievements.

Sadly, the Luftwaffe didn't necessarily agree, or maybe their target maps failed to highlight William John's earthenware Pig, and on the 15th of January 1941 a careless Bomb-aimer (Bombenschuetze) let drop a stick of things that go bang in the night, not only rattling the casements and doing untold damage to the bandstand but also decapitating the poor boar.

Derby was, regrettably, boarless, until 2005. In this year a sculptor and engineer called Alex Paxton created a bronze statue of the boar, which has replaced the terracotta one. Oh Joy, we all say, and partly in gratitude to Mr Paxton, who did the thing for nothing except the cost of materials. It is a magnificent statue, and considerably more durable, being of metal. We are now friends with the Luftwaffe, so things are looking rosy.

Do you remember, about 467 words ago, we were talking about Florentine traditions? Well, without any prompting, the good people of Derby have come over all Italian, and taken to patting the nose of the boar, as they go past it. It was this that made the replacing of the nose necessary, all those years ago, so presumably Mr Paxton, being aware of nasal wear and tear, has built a rather more durable one than did either Pietro Tacca or Mr Coffee. History is recorded so that we can learn from it.

Frankly, the original bronze lasted 235 years, give or take, so there's no need to start panicking just yet, and we British are not quite so passionate in our snout-patting as the Italians - well, we aren't about patting other things, so it's a reasonable assumption. That being the case, the statue should be there a long time yet, for millions to enjoy, and no doubt the boar, were it sentient, would enjoy having its olfactory organ fondled on a regular basis. You can't ask for more than that.

Derby Ram

It takes little imagination to work out how the name evolved, since rams are notorious for head-butting things, although, to be fair, some Millwall supporters have a similar reputation.

WE live in a world where the simple word 'Ram' has had a good few meanings. Once upon a time, when the cannon reigned supreme, and every good man and true had the ambition to sink a French Man O' War, the ram was the long pole thing with a soft head on it, the same size as the bore of the gun. It was used to shove wadding, gunpowder and the like down the muzzle of the offending (and, indeed, offensive) weapon, prior to singing three choruses of Land and Hope and Glory, two of Hearts of Oak, and giving Nelson, our Nel, three Huzzahs.

After this, the rum was broken out, and the entire crew spliced mainbraces and so forth.

Go back a bit earlier than that, a scant couple of thousand years, and the ram was used to break down city walls, smash the gates, force a way in through the fortifications and thus slaughter everybody, in the name of civilisation, prior to three choruses of something arcane in Greek, then breaching a barrel of retsina and wondering what on earth a mainbrace was, is, or will be.

It takes little or no imagination to work out how the name evolved, since rams are notorious for head-butting things, although, to be fair, some Millwall supporters have a similar reputation.

This was fine until some clown invented the computer, and the acronym held sway. Holds sway, actually, because we are still stuck with initials all over the place, ever since IBM gave us the ATM and FDDI, and then it went mad with AMD, PCI, ISP, ADSL, BIO, FSB, USB, CPU, ALU, CDM and, of course RAM. Random Access Memory, and since the average ram is sufficiently un-educated to worry about most of the things that humans do, its memory can afford to be both random and only sporadically accessible.

This information holds good throughout the entire civilised earth, and quite a few places that are slightly less civilised, such as Milton Keynes. However, Derbyshire is immune from such shenanigans, for it has its own Ram. Obviously, there are a couple of computers in Derbyshire, you can't cobble together jet engines without them these days. If your SFC is 1.195 lb/(lbf.h), or 33.8 g/(kN.S), with an effective exhaust velocity of 29,553, which is what is going to get you from here to New York without having to swim part of the way, you can see where an abacus might cramp your style a bit. The ramifications are endless.

Derbyshire has a ram in its county crest, which is working hard at assisting a stag to hold up a shield, with a wyvern balanced atop. Mention stags in crests, though, and most thought goes north of the border, to the Hielands and Glens o' Bonny Scotland. Mention The Wyvern, and those that don't say "Wot?" will associate it with the Midland Railway, which, as every schoolboy knows, was based in Derby.

This leaves our male of the species Ovis Aries. Derby City Council, not to be outdone, also has a crest, but this time the ram is at the top, being held up on its shield by the same stag, but another one has been drafted in to assist. The Wyvern has gone somewhere else, presumably by train.

As well as its heraldry, Derby, both shire and city, are proud of their football club, Derby County, which also, you will be unsurprised to know, has a ram on its crest. Strangely, though, Derby County were very slow in adopting their badge, and despite being one of the original dozen clubs to make up the Football League, in eighteen hundred and frozen to death, it didn't have a permanent badge until 1926, and that didn't last long.

They had another ram for the 1946 Cup Final, as a result of which they won, beating Charlton Athletic, who were obviously not as athletic as they should have been, and then it quietly disappeared until 1971. Enter, stage left, one Brian Clough, a powerhouse, or similar expression, who, amongst other things, reinstated the ram, but this time, not merely a head. The ram was depicted as sideways on, ready to charge (football clubs always are, one way or the other) and dubbed the 'Snorting Ram'. It has faced right, it has faced left, it has no doubt gone off on the rampage, but it's still there.

But where did all this rammery originate from? The answer is dotted all over the fields of the county. Large, woolly lumps, that will end up as Fair-Isle sweaters, or served with a few peas and a roast spud or two.

Wander the by-lanes of the Peak District in spring and you will see hordes of townies gawping at the lambs, and making 'Aaahh' noises. It will be pointed out by all and sundry that they are gorgeous; look at that little one gambolling, don't they look lovely, and then at seven o'clock the pubs and restaurants are full of the same good folk, ordering their lamb chops, lamb casserole, lamb shank or lamb tikka masala.

Some, it must be said, look like mutton dressed as lamb, and others, usually their offspring, look like lamb dressed as offal, but then, teenage fashion always was a challenge to long-suffering parents. Incidentally, it is not uncommon for the child to order a lentil burger, then harangue their parents for the entire meal about their barbarism, cruelty, feelinglessness (their word, not mine) heartlessness and so on. Fear not, for in a few years, they too will be getting outside a lamb madras, if they are male and macho, or a rack of lamb with mint sauce, if they are less bothered about looking hard. Maybe it bothers them, at such a tender age, that there are more sheep than humans in the county. It perhaps makes them feel sheepish.

Surprisingly, since we have already noted the prevalence of things alcoholic within the field, so to speak, of folklore, there are very few pubs celebrating the ram. There is a Ram Inn in Derby itself, and the Derby Tup in Chesterfield, tup being an old word for our woolly hero. It's also a verb, but that is left to your fertile imagination.

That appears to be your lot, unless there's one lurking in some quiet hamlet that only a few locals and the odd CAMRA member know about, and some of them can be very odd indeed. And yet, the Army have taken the ram on board in big style. The First Battalion, the Worcester and Sherwood Foresters, whose memorial is at Crich Stand, have had a ram as their mascot since 1858, when one of the now constituent regiments was the 95th Derbshire Regiment.

Each ram has been known as Private Derby, with, to date, none of them having made the grade to Lance Corporal, which, some believe, puts the Army on the horns of a dilemma. However, the vast majority of rams seem to be quite happy to be a member of such a fine regiment, and do not complain.

As you would expect, each has had a service number, the first being, hardly surprisingly, No. 1, and the present one No. 28, and they are very proud of their lineage. Each is a Swaledale ram from the estate of the Dukes of Devonshire, whose seat is, as you would imagine, in Derbyshire, namely Chatsworth.

On parade, Pte Derby wears a coat of scarlet, with Lincoln green and gold facings, which bears the Indian Mutiny Medal, as well as the General Service Medal, for many a ram has seen active service, presumably manning the ramparts. On his forehead is a silver plate bearing the regimental badge, and there is a silver protector over each of his horns.

The Army are not daft, and this is to stop acts of insubordination, whereby the clothing of the Ram Major, his guide and mentor, do not get damaged. The Ram Orderly is of a lower station in life, and whilst it is less important should he get a quick going over, for the sake of symmetry, both horns are similarly adorned.

The Derby Ram, or Tup - call it what you will - is also a folk song and the subject of a playlet, performed by many a mummer and guiser, throughout the county. This will be dealt with under a separate heading, to save the reader getting information overload. You wouldn't want to feel that you are banging your head against a brick wall. You would only accuse us of ramming it down your throat.

Derby Tup

He was not a small ram, being in the order of ten yards tall, give or take an inch, and the wool was so high that eagles made their nests in it.

IF you have made the mistake of just glancing through this magnificent tome, instead of reading it through, page after page, in an orderly manner, you may well have already seen the bit on Mummers and Guisers.

Admittedly, it does sound a bit like an American pop group from the 1970s, but there is little can be done about this. Do not start thinking in terms of Mummer Cass, you will only confuse yourself. Be honest, though, you originally confused yourself by skip-reading, which you have been warned about before.

You were on the point of saying "You cannot have a piece about traditional English plays, in a book about Derbyshire, and not include The Derby Tup". Your next move was donning your mac and wellies, grabbing your brolly and going back to the bookshop in high dudgeon to beat on the desk for a bit, and then demand your money back. You have just been saved endless embarrassment. Read on.

The Derby Tup is a folk poem, often set to music, which tells the story of a singular ram, from the good city of Derby. If it was from Birmingham, they'd call it The Brummagem Tup, which, you have to admit, stands to reason. Incidentally, in almost every case where you hear that particular phrase, you can be almost certain that somebody is going to say something utterly unreasonable.

This Ram, Sir, was the finest Ram, Sir, that ever was fed on hay. He was not a small ram, though, being in the order of ten yards tall, give or take an inch, and the wool was so high that eagles made their nests in it, despite the fact that nobody has seen an eagle anywhere near Derbyshire for quite some considerable time.

Its wool, on the other hand, reached to the ground, and was worth a bob or two - well, £40,000, and as we have said before, who are we to argue? The space between the ram's horns was only a scant six feet or so, Sir, this being the span of a man's arms, in which they build a pulpit. Presumably the parson wished to preach to his flock!

Also, this fine and magnificent beast had as many teeth as there are men in a regiment, and the tongue between them would have fed said regiment. As you would expect, Sir, this is one large beastie, and it had a tail, as rams do, over exactly ten miles and an ell.

Now, unless you are a Scrabble fan, and therefore likely to know a few useless words that went out with the Ark, you will be a-scratching of your head, and asking yourself what the ell is. It is 45 inches, or if you are more used to this foreign metric stuff, 114.3 cm, thus making the entire tail 17.0487 kilometres.

Sadly, but inevitably, the butcher did what butchers do, and the poor Tup was no more. As it happens, nor was the butcher, because, this being a somewhat larger than average animal, he drowned in the blood, but we need not dwell on this, nor the fact that the small boys of the town begged the eyeballs to use as footballs.

As with any traditional rhyme, there are local variations, some of which will not appear on these pages, because we are rather hoping that you will buy this book for Granny, as a present, and the last thing we want is our readership having an attack of the vapours.

Also, there have been occasions where the dimensions of the Tup have been exaggerated, which we have tried to avoid. We only wish to bring you the truth, the whole truth and nothing but the truth. We take this commission very seriously, and you can take everything you have read between these covers as being absolutely true. As sure as I'm sitting on this thirty-foot ram, Sir.

Derbyshire Cheese

It is only made in the village of Hartington, which has the best cheesery in the world, although there is a certain amount of bias in that statement.

WHAT do Leicester, Gloucester, Oxford and Bath have in common? Simple, you say, dead easy, they are all county towns, piece of cake, where's my $64,000? Ah, yes, well, you are part way right, but only part way.

If the town of Lanark were thrown in to the melting pot, would it help or confuse? Let's make it all even easier - Stilton, Wensleydale, Caerphilly (or more accurately, Caerffili), Cheshire and Cheddar. Got it, yet? Oh, come on! All right, one final clue: "Wise man's horse race is cheesy in the Midlands".

But what has all this got to do with Derbyshire? Well, the very fact that there are three different cheeses associated with the county. The most obvious one, of course, is Derby, which is better known with Sage, and which, oddly, may have nothing to do with Derbyshire whatsoever. Having said that, the only people that make such a claim are from Yorkshire, so we can perhaps ignore it. It is only on the grounds that the largest manufacturer is in Yorkshire, but history points to the fact that it was invented, if that's the right word for cheese, in Derbyshire during the 17th century. Originally, it was only made for use at harvest-time, holidays and other celebrations, so it is a very special cheese indeed. It is also an interesting green colour, and green cheeses are exceptionally rare, except, as everybody knows, that the moon is made of it. This was a well-known fact long before Yorkshire's only astronaut, Helen Sharman, went anywhere near the place.

Sage Derby is a cow's milk cheese, which may well have had the sage added, not for taste or colour, but as a curative. In the 17th century, you couldn't just nip down to Boot's for some proprietary brand, so you could get it in your cheese. Apparently it was good for sweating, to aid digestion, depression, anxiety, liver disorders, laryngitis and tonsillitis. Inevitably, the experts recommend eating it with a plum wine or a Shiraz. We are in no position to argue, even were we daft enough to do so.

A lesser known cheese is Buxton Blue, which, unbelievably, comes from Buxton and is... well... blue. It is also mandated under the Protected Designation of Origin laws as being exclusive to Buxton, which means that if you want to eat it with a Cornish Pasty, or some Cumberland Sausage, it won't matter where the pie or banger were made, but you can rest assured that your cheese is truly local, and only made with milk from certain parts of Derbyshire, Nottinghamshire or Staffordshire. It is a deep russet colour, lightly veined with blue, and a distant cousin, if you can imagine such a thing, of the Stilton cheese. Very nice with a glass of port - or two! By the way, if you go into a shop and ask for Buxton Blue, beware, for there is also a geranium with the same name. Whilst some geraniums, or possibly gerania, are edible, others are toxic. It is as well to be aware of these things.

But, hold hard, there is yet another cheese, also a blue, and also with Protected Origin, that being the Dovedale. Now, Dovedale is a dale, on the River Dove, really, and the cheese is named after it. Again, it is related to Stilton, but is not as well known. Indeed, it is only made in the village of Hartington, which has the best cheesery in the world, although there is a certain amount of bias in that statement. It is best eaten with a lighter wine than other blue cheeses and Beaujolais seems to be the favourite. However, unlike Buxton Blue, the milk can be obtained from the same sources, but also from cows resident in Shropshire and Cheshire "if exceptional circumstances arise". Answers on a postcard, please.

It is very easy to think of cheese-making as being a wonderfully rural occupation, done by bonny, cheery, red-cheeked ladies sitting on three-legged stools, in between their knitting, but to dispel the myth, Dovedale cheese is better known in the industry as being of PAI Specification AS06. However, it matters not one jot what Euro-bureaucrats call it, it is superb, and there is nowhere better on the planet to eat. Indeed, nowhere else.

'Wise man's horse race is cheesy in the Midlands' should be a clue to the county's 17th century invention

Derbyshire Dry Stone Walls

The limestone used in the walls of the Peak goes some wonderful colours when wet, so get out your waterproofs and go to have a look.

SOME facts you cannot be expected to know, despite the fact that, by purchasing this book alone, you have demonstrated your intelligence, erudition, taste, judgement and, no doubt, good looks.

One of those facts is that your current correspondent's wife's maiden name was Waller, for her family did exactly that. They made walls, albeit in days of old, when knights were bold, and before we all got herded in to Victorian factories to get smothered in oil.

My father-in-law, George, who spent much of his life in Castleton, was a first-rate mechanic, who got his taste for machinery helping cyclists at his uncle's cafe, in about 1925. Originally, his love grew from being responsible for taking the cyclists of the time a drink of orange squash, a towel and a piece of soap, but his skills grew with age, and before car manufacturers started putting micro-chips in everything, he could make an engine talk.

As far as I know, he never actually built a dry stone wall, although such was the way of life then, it is always possible. It is known that he helped repair some, which are still standing. He seemed to be able to turn his hand to just about anything, without any seeming effort. As one to whom the phrase 'DIY' means bandages, leaking arteries, lost tools and machinery in a more parlous state than before I started, I have learned the hard way not to attempt anything more technical than changing a light bulb, and then under wifely supervision. I would have made a dreadful dry stone waller.

You can't help but notice that Derbyshire has dry stone walls instead of hedges, which gives the landscape a unique look. The reason is lost in the mists of history, but it goes something like this: During the Dark Ages, so called because there were so many Knights, the Anglo-Saxons settled in the lowland areas, because Saxony is pretty flat, and they didn't know how to cope with hills. Also, if you have to drag your days out farming uphill, it gets sweaty and the Anglo-Saxons were not as daft as archaeologists would have you believe.

To be fair, their agricultural techniques suited lowland terrain better. During the medieval period, more upland areas got to be used, especially in ecclesiastical settlements, and they rather liked their religion, then. In particular the Cistercians liked dry stone walls, although the reason why the White Monks were so keen has been lost to us. Perhaps it is what they were used to in France, and it just became a habit. Anyway, even to this day, when monks are not an everyday sight, in the upland areas of Britain fields are often separated by walls rather than hedges. There is also the point that, certainly in Derbyshire, where the weather can be wilder and woollier than the native sheep, a hedge is not as durable as a wall, and is less use for hiding behind from the wind if you are a sheep. Don't let anybody tell you that sheep are stupid. When you find out, and you are just about to, that the breed of sheep indigenous to the county is the Derbyshire Gritstone, you see the parallel.

Hardy, robust, aristocratic, strong, alert, agile, neatly proportioned, compact, strong-placed shoulders and with good looks. An interesting sentence, and not an extract from your current correspondent's CV, although it could be. No, it is a description of the Derbyshire Gritstone sheep. It has been around since 1770, and it isn't likely to go away, unless we all magically turn in to vegetarians overnight, so it is therefore traditional, and worthy of inclusion. You may well wonder what it is doing within a piece on dry-stone walling, and the answer is, because it is usually within dry stone walls. Sometimes we can't see the wood for the trees.

This book will not tell you how to build a dry stone wall, since to do so would require many hours spent on Google, which you might as well do yourself, if that is your wont. You might be better off getting in the experts, who will build a wall that will last for the remainder of our lifetimes, and a long way beyond that. It is reputed that many of the walls in the Peak District are hundreds of years old. The other reason for not giving massive detail is that, having already admitted to not being of a practical bent, any advice given wouldn't be worth a light.

Suffice it to say that, although dry stone walling goes back many a long year, and there are walls across the globe that are claimed to be from the 3rd Century BC, Derbyshire's are an attractive feature of the county, partly because of the colour of the stone. Most of us want to curl up by the fire when it is raining, but the limestone used in the walls of the Peak goes some wonderful colours when wet, so get out your waterproofs and go to have a look. Alternatively, you could go out on a dry day and take a watering can with you, but you might end up in lengthy discussions with a farmer who frankly wouldn't believe a word of what you are saying. Rain, as it happens, is fairly plentiful in the Peak District, so you shouldn't have too much of a problem laying your hands upon some.

The only other place where simple walls can be so beautiful is in the bluegrass area of Kentucky, but there is a down-side. You will not see any astoundingly good-looking, aristocratic sheep.

Derbyshire Executions

Once the criminal had been snuffed out, it was customary to leave the body in a metal cage for all to see and thus be deterred. Fat lot of good that did, mind.

THE current population, or at least, the population the last time that anybody counted, was about sixty million, six hundred thousand. The figure is actually given as 60,609,153, but this is a bit of a joke, because within 20 minutes of the numbers even being recorded, 934 women had given birth to a single child, 89 to twins, seven to triplets, and one to octuplets, although I admit that this information is from the editor of the Daily Sport.

By the same token, a goodly number had shuffled off this mortal coil, several dying of shock at the increase in population, usually those who had been around in 1901 when the population was a scant 41,609,091. However, what is a cause for concern is the population density in certain areas, and since this precious wee tome is about Derbyshire, there are no prizes for guessing where we are worrying about today.

Derbyshire covers an area of a rather convenient 555 square miles, although this wasn't always the case. Various bits have been pinched over the years, usually by a voracious Yorkshire, which is ever on the qui vive for more ratepayers.

Within that 555 square miles, there live a contented and happy 93,278 people, give or take the odd octuplet. These are typified by those who work for Rolls Royce, those who work on the land, those who write pointless books about the Peak District and those who are employed by the local council. As you would imagine, some of those who work for the council also produce pointless books, or have a couple of sheep hanging around the place.

Now, those who are reading this expansive and scholarly work will already have taken their calculator down from the shelf, blown the dust off, and worked out that this means a figure of only 258 people per square mile. Compare this with a total of 34,565 per square mile in Greater London, 3,732 in Sheffield, or 9,880 in Manchester and you start to see a disparity. Why?

Does this mean that Derbyshire is less desirable than the capital, or the other two cities cited? Far from it. The reasons are darker than that.

Be honest, if you lived in a 37th floor flat, which would you rather look out on? With a choice of the 37th floor flat in the block next door (and you have to hope they have net curtains), or a vista over fields of sheep and cattle to nearby Mam Tor, or Mam Nick, despite the latter sounding like the local lock-up, there isn't much of a choice to make. Well, unless you're a Peeping Tom, that is. There is no known record of sheep living on the 37th floor, although that might be because of the difficulty reaching the buttons in the lift.

And yet, more of us live in the towns than out in the sticks, and not only because of wanting to be within walking distance of the chip shop. The reasons why are dead simple - literally. The reason why Derbyshire is so sparsely populated, with sheep outnumbering humans most of the time, is that it has a strange habit of bumping people off. Well, had, to be more accurate; the custom seems to have died off, so to speak. Allow me to explain, before somebody has an ancient law repealed, and I end up being taken off to the gallows.

Derbyshire has had a bit of a problem with witches, or indeed, anybody with a dark coloured cat, so it stands to reason that they had to be got rid of, although the ultimate fate of the moggies is unrecorded. The British having a soft spot for animals, there may well have been a Witches and Warlocks Cat Retirement home, complete with comfortable broomsticks to sit upon and possibly a Spell Cell.

We are an immensely compassionate nation. Except where some ratbag stole a sheep, of course, which was a surefire method of testing the quality of the rope made at Castleton, or at least, a short quantity thereof. It appears that it was of an excellent standard, although there seem to be no reports from recipients, which can be taken as being positive. Nicking somebody else's loaf was another good method, although, with a loaf costing a penny, and having to pay the hangman three bob, it was hardly cost-effective. However, it was an almost daily occurrence, being known as the Nine O'Clock Noose.

Murderers, felons, blackguards, ne'er-do-wells, vagabonds, loafers, sluggards, malcontents, wastrels, fly-by-nights, delinquents, vagrants and the like got their come-uppance, as did those who refused to testify in court, which seems a bit harsh.

"Do you have anything to say to this court?"

"No, me lud."

"Oh good. Kill 'im!"

The method of executing those who decided to remain silent was barbaric in the extreme. Frankly, I was going to explain it, but I came over all wobbly at the thought, and it is extraordinarily difficult to type and be sick at the same time. If you wish to know more, please help yourself - Mr Google is only too happy to fulfill your ghoulish cravings, and give you all the sickening details of how somebody was Pressed to Death.

Other methods were a bit less revolting, although, if you're on the wrong end of it, I don't suppose it would make much difference if you were hanged, and if you had been, whether you were drawn and quartered. The only thing you can say in its favour is that it was quicker than being burnt to death. In most normal cases, though, a simple hanging was good enough. Dash it all, it's practically a custom, doncherknow. So much less messy than beheading, what!

Derbyshire had to go one step better, though. Once the criminal had been snuffed out, it was customary to leave the body in a metal cage for all to see and thus be deterred. Fat lot of good that did, mind. The last gibbetting in the county was one Anthony Lingard, who was hung in chains at Wardlow, and 11 years later, his brother committed, or is accused of committing - records vary - an equally unpleasant crime within view of his late brother.

A final word on the evil custom, and a sad reflection on man's inhumanity to man. One kind gentleman, a member of Sir Francis Drake's voyage to South America, wrote the following:

"After having walked 11 hours without having traced the print of a human foot, to my great comfort and delight, I saw a man hanging upon a gibbet; my pleasure at the cheering prospect was inexpressible, for it convinced me that I was in a civilized country." Quite.

One poor unfortunate earns my sympathy. It is not recorded what dastardly deed he carried out, but he was transported for the privilege. Somehow, he returned, and as a punishment, he was hanged, in 1757. Just think, today, he'd make a fortune selling his story to the papers, and would probably finish up with his own television show.

To put this in perspective, the times were cruel, and executions almost commonplace. Of the 74 people hanged in Derby alone, between 1742 and 1837, some of the crimes were by today's standards pitiful - picking pockets, horse-stealing, counterfeiting and housebreaking. Again, the path to stardom, in our more liberal age.

The last public execution in Derby was on April 11th, 1862, one Richard Thorley. In 1846 a hanging had attracted a crowd of 20,000, but another in 1861, and get that date into perspective, it wasn't *that* long ago, a crowd of 50,000 flocked to see George Smith die, with special trains being laid on. Convinced you are in a civilized country?

Of course, the other side of the coin is that nobody has to fork out for food for years, rope isn't that expensive, there is always some barbarian prepared to don the black mask - and probably for nothing - and you don't get repeat offenders. The fact that you are treating murder with murder is a small consideration, and if you read the Letters page of some local papers, hanging should be brought back for parking offences, whistling out of tune or coming from the wrong village.

Beheading is reserved for those from neighbouring counties. That's why it has been included as a tradition. Good grief, it was good enough for Mary Queen of Scots, of whom it can be said that if she had actually done all the tapestries it is claimed she did, she would have to have lived to the age of 183. To get to stay in all the places that claim she did, just a tad longer. You just can't believe people would tell such lies. There's only one answer: hang 'em!

Derbyshire Highwaymen

In the 21st century each highwayman would have to be licensed by the state and given an identifying plastic badge to wear around his neck.

DERBYSHIRE has a great tradition of highwaymen. There are none left now. We do not need them, since we now have motorway service stations. There are only three in Derbyshire, but they have robbed more people than Dick Turpin and his mates. The only difference is that Turpin had the decency to wear a mask.

For objects of hatred out on the road, there is always White Van Man or the suave individual in white shirt, flash cuff-links, red braces and over-shiny shoes, in his expensive piece of German ironmongery, sitting about three inches off your back bumper.

Of course, now that "highwayman" is not an option when today's children go to the careers advisor, unlike the millions of opportunities for unemployment in the entertainment sector, recruiting has fallen off of late.

There is also the fact that standing in front of a 44-tonner hurtling down the A623 with a brace of flintlock pistols, and shouting "Stand and Deliver" is not particularly effective. It tends to shorten many a promising career, never mind the difficulty of getting hold of a lace-bedecked tricorn hat.

We mentioned Dick Turpin earlier. Turpin was not the gallant highwayman of myth, and since he was not a Derbyshireman, he will get short shrift here. Suffice it to say that he was a petty thief, poacher, cattle thief, murderer and all round bad egg. He did not make the legendary ride from York to London, because the best horse in the world couldn't possibly do it at an average speed of 18mph - your everyday 44-tonner struggles. But, it seems that the ride was done by somebody else.

Of course, it is also claimed that nearly all of his dastardly deeds were performed between Huntingdon and York, and that Derbyshire never got a look in. Not so, for 'tis said that he visited the Bull i' Thorn pub, and indeed, that 'is ghost do 'aunt it, of a quiet night, Sirree.

All of which makes you wonder why the average self-respecting spook wouldn't stay in York, and save himself a lot of aggravation. Having said that, if a life is practically all fiction, the death might as well be, too. Whilst we're in the Bull i' Thorn, one Joseph Millner, highwayman, was born here, but again, he doesn't seem to have been particularly brilliant at it. He got his collar felt several times, and finished up making a hangman's day on August 14th, 1751.

The incredible ride is attributed to one John Nevison, who, so successful and gentlemanly was he, was awarded the soubriquet "Swift Nick" by no lesser a personage than King Charles II. The rest of the story is fictional as well, but somehow, a bit like Robin Hood, you want to believe it, so believe it we shall.

Swift Nick came originally from Wortley, in what is now South Yorkshire, but it is known that he committed some of his robberies in that county's southern neighbour. There is a record of him in the Newgate Calendar, a strongly moralistic tome which appeared some time between about 1750 and 1774. Part of the poor boy's problem was that he fell in with "canting beggars, pilgrims of the earth, the offspring of Cain, vagabonds and wanderers, fit companions for such as made a trade of idleness and roguery." No wonder he went off the rails. In mitigation, it is claimed that he never used violence against any of his victims, and he was known as "the glamorous highwayman." It is unknown how glamorous those who had just had their money nicked, as it were, thought he was.

Even if Mr Nevison operated elsewhere, Black Harry didn't. Harold was known to have worked the roads around Longstone, Wardlow, Tideswell and Bakewell, making a lucrative living from the pack-mule trains. Lucrative, but he did not need a retirement plan, because the Castleton Bow Street Runners, a wonderful name, cut his career short, and shortly thereafter his life insurance matured suddenly, on the Gallows Tree at Wardlow.

Other highwaymen operated on the stretch of road between Derby and Chesterfield, which, by one of those strange quirks of fate, is where you will find at least one of the service stations referred to earlier. The road from Chesterfield down to Baslow was another favourite for The Gentlemen, and there is still a pub there called the Highwayman.

There is also a fictional highwayman, who roamed the area around Brassing Moor, by the name of Beau Brocade, and wouldn't you love to have a moniker like that in your passport? The inestimable Beau, real name Captain Jack Bathurst of His Majesty's White Dragoons, was an all-round good guy, who robbed from the rich and gave to the poor, which rings a faint bell somewhere. He appears in a book by Baroness Orczy, from 1907, whose full name is Emma Magdolna Rozalia Maria Jozefa Borbala "Emmuska" Orczy de Orczi, which is a book in itself.

As far as we know, there were no highwaywomen working around Derbyshire, although there must have been some. Bit of a shame, really, because some of the ones who are recorded elsewhere have the most magnificent names. The two we must include, despite their probably never having even heard of the county, much less been here, are Mary Frith, otherwise known as Moll Cutpurse, and the superbly named Bonnie Grizelda. They are included out of pure jealousy!

Sadly, those days are long gone, if only because in the 21st century each highwayman would have to be licensed by the state and given an identifying plastic badge to wear around his neck which makes the art of detection somewhat superfluous.

He would have to go on courses for Health and Safety, Flintlock Design and Construction, he'd need an NVQ in Black Powder Handling, Correct Deployment of Face Masks, and then be allocated his own stretch of road. There would be triangular warning signs, with tricorn-clad individuals in flowing cloaks, and white lines painted to delineate the sphere of operations.

All horses would have to have registrations, and you can hardly go about your business on something called 5525 NK, when previously you had Black Bess.

Every year, the bloke from the revenue would be round, with a form containing such headings as "Coaches Robbed" or "Jewels Taken" (not including commercial jewels or rhinestones) as per the Jewels Act 2007 rev 2009, para 3 sub-para iii)". If you were really good, you might finish up paying VAT.

You would be subject to speed limits, which is a bit unfair when you are on your bay gelding, and the Old Bill have got a souped-up Land Rover. You'd need pretty good health insurance, too. Leaving aside the question of the risks attached to wandering around with a couple of loaded pistols stuck in your belt, it gets pretty cold and wet up in the Peak. You're almost bound to get a cold, and then where would you be? Stand in front of someone and shout "Your Bunny or Your Life!", anything could happen.

Frankly, the romance has gone out of it.

"Highwayman" is not an option when today's children go to see the careers advisor

Derbyshire Morris Dancing

Don't let anybody kid you that this is just a disparate bunch of blokes waving sticks and hankies in time to a bit of music.

THOSE of a certain age, on hearing the word "Morris", think of the car manufacturer. How could they forget the Morris 8, the Morris 10, the Morris 1000, better known as a Moggie, and other iconic names.

The Company eventually disappeared, ignominiously, having become part of the British Motor Corporation, which became the British Leyland Motor Corporation, which became British Leyland, which coughed up blood for a short while, then died, wheezing.

In 1984 the last Morris car ever, the Morris Ital, was made. You never see one, which is a bit on the odd side, because you still see the Moggie, with its lovely, burbly exhaust note, and distinctive gearbox whine. They are driven either by enthusiasts with beards or little old ladies who bought theirs new, and have run up a massive total of 19,000 miles in 38 years, having named it "George" or some such.

The company was started by one William Morris, which does not come as much of a surprise, but he must not be confused with William Morris the artist, architect, designer, writer, poet and Pre-Raphaelite. The multi-talented William (the elder) died in 1896, rather before the internal combustion became as popular as it now is, but he is sadly remembered for just one thing. All that writing, some superb poetry, imaginative buildings, translations of great works (including from Icelandic), paintings that people still stand in front of for hours, and some half-wit will say, "Oh yeah, I know about 'im, 'e invented wallpaper!" If you meet such a person, no jury would convict you.....

So, where is the connection between this and Morris Dancing, you ask? Answer: there isn't one, but you can never tell when you might need to know about wallpapering cars, or whatever it was, so it stands on its own merits.

Morris Dancing has been around considerably longer than cars, and probably wallpaper, which is known to have been around in 1509, so poor old Bill gets it in the neck again.

There is a claim for Morris Dancing in 1448, but it has been disputed. This seems a bit heartless, to chuck unfounded accusations at a tradition that can't answer back, even if it wanted to after all these years. Nobody disputes wallpaper, after all, except one or two very sad individuals who should get out more.

The name Morris also causes many an argument in the snug of an evening, at which point most others wander in to the other bar for a game of darts, or to look at the wall, which is probably more interesting. Especially if it is papered. If you care why Morris is called Morris, or if it really began in the same year that Queen's College Cambridge was founded, this is not the book for you. Actually, it is possible that it was originally Moorish Dancing, and it was certainly around early enough for Cromwell to ban it, along with just about anything else that people enjoyed.

There are about a dozen Morris sides to be found in Derbyshire, in such places as Winster, Long Eaton, Derby, Chapel-en-le-Frith, Chesterfield and Ripley, but they do not all do the same things, which is where this could get complicated. However, now that you've got this far, is it worth quitting? Bear with me.

There are different sorts of Morris, as you would expect. Since it is not just restricted to Derbyshire, you could hardly expect all the sides, as they are called, to do the same thing. To illustrate, Winster Morris Men perform all their own dances, which are unique. Among them are such dances as The Taddington Morris, which had been performed in Taddington in 1931, the Queen's Morris, to commemorate their own Winster Queen, the Rose of Taddington, as a memorial to a former dancer, and Flag Waving, which celebrates Winster being twinned with Monterubbiano, in Italy. Their favourite finale is the Winster Gallop.

Whilst the Morris side are dancing, the King and Queen preside, as is only right, and there are the Jester and the Witch to keep the crowd amused. Spellbound? A tiny little detail, but each dancer wears their own unique rosette, although they are all of the same basic pattern. It is the attention to such things that makes Morris so appealing.

Ripley's Morris Men perform all over the world, which rather makes you wonder what the people of Lyons, say, would make of it. If you are from Lyons, please send your answers on a postcard...

Ripley also have a support team, in the shape of The Fool, Molly and Horace the Unicorn, who no doubt get in the way of the Men as they try and perform their traditional Cotswold Morris. However, if you'd rather see traditional Welsh Border Morris, a group called Freaks in the Peaks are worth looking for. Welsh Border Morris involves such things as blue-painted faces, decorated top hats, and dances called things like Tinner's Rabbit, Welly Boot and Twiglet.

Don't let anybody kid you that this is just a disparate bunch of blokes waving sticks and hankies in time to a bit of music, and for two reasons. Firstly, Freaks have ladies dancing as well as the men, and secondly, you only have to look at the directions for each individual dance to see how complicated it is. So are the costumes. Compare the blacked-out faces and darker clothing of the Powder Kegs Morris Men of Whaley Bridge with the predominant white of, say, the Cotswold Morris sides, and there is a world of difference. Then bear in mind that there is a form of Morris called Derbyshire Morris, which is a processional dance, and usually done without bells, and you start to realise how complex the world of Morris Dancing can be.

Other forms of Morris include Clog Dancing, and once again, Derbyshire won't let you down. Whaley Bridge, again, whose inhabitants obviously like to keep fitter than the rest of we couch potatoes. They also do Broom Dancing, which most gentlemen think is the sole preserve of their mother-in-law, but not so.

Stone Monkey Sword Dancers have everything to do with swords, for they dance with them - if they didn't, you couldn't really call it a sword dance and get away with it, and the swords get woven into all kinds of strange shapes, rarely with the removal of fingers, although it is a fair bet that there is a certain amount of swearing in rehearsal.

This form of sword dancing, known as rapper, and not to be confused with pop singers who cannot sing, and therefore chant the first thing that comes in to their tiny little minds, was started in the pit villages of Northumberland, and it is great that a Derbyshire village should be keeping it going. Why Stone Monkey? Well, why not? If you wish to see about 15 different explanations, some a shade too indelicate for these august pages, their website is one of the funniest I have ever seen - funnier than mine, for which I hate them, but I wish them well.

Look, it would be perfectly possible to rabbit on for ever about the different sorts of dancing found in the county, but it would be a poor substitute for actually witnessing it for yourself, which is what is recommended. You can look at pictures, you can gawp at slightly fuzzy films on the interweb thingy, you can try all manner of strange things, but you can't beat going to see it. And hear it.

Of course, if it is raining heavily, and you still want something to do, you might go to the National Motor Museum, which was started by William Morris, later Lord Nuffield. The disadvantage is that it is not in Derbyshire, but in Beaulieu, which is down South somewhere (SO42 7ZN, for those with Satnav). You'll have a great day out, but it won't be half as noisy, or half as much of a laugh. And it certainly won't be one tenth as traditional.

*Derbyshire Morris is a processional dance,
and usually done without bells.*

Derbyshire Mummers & Guisers

The sword fight is done with as much swashbuckling as Errol Flynn could ever have mustered, but with more convincing accents.

TO be frank, some of our mummers are better known as guisers, and some were even called pace-eggers, but it doesn't make much difference. The end result is the same.
Of course, if you happen to be reading this in Dresden, say, or Hanover, you will know that mumming is from a German word for wearing a mask (der sich vermummt) and was used by the Brothers Grimm, although a long time after it was first employed in the fourteenth century.
As with all unusual words, there are a hundred explanations, most of which are pretty improbable, but this one seems the most plausible. One source says that it was from the French, but our language is Indo-Germanic, we are Anglo-Saxon, and I wouldn't imagine the Norman French would have allowed such jollity, especially since it was all to do with Celtic fertility rites. Now, of course, it is a tradition, and very few men dressing up in strange costumes and reciting words first coined hundreds of years ago are going to worry about their testosterone levels.
The main theme of any mumming play seems to be a combat between the hero and the villain, in which the hero gets killed. Centuries later the late, great Spike Milligan used the same device in the Goon Show. "You rotten swine, you deaded me!" quoth Bluebottle, every week, but he would be back the following week to be deaded once again. The only difference is that in the mumming plays, the hero is brought back to life by a quack doctor - a phrase it is inadvisable to use near any of the county's first-class hospitals.
Of course, some of the mummers who started all this off are no longer with us, if only because there is one known script from the 1790s in the Ron Nurse collection. There are any number from the nineteenth century. The earliest known reference was in 1377, when Prince Richard, later Richard II, was entertained at Kennington. It doesn't matter one jot if there were pre-Christian fertility references or not, because the lad would have been ten at the time.
So, where does one go if one wishes to be mummed to, or should that be mummed at? There are choices, of course. Longford will welcome you with open arms, as will Parwich, Ripley, Tideswell and Winster. If you wish to see all of them, it is going to be a very busy Christmas period for you, because this is when it all happens.
Paganism and religious traditions have long gone hand-in-hand. Glossop Guizers (the spelling seems to be pretty random) started in 2003, and although their events are rather

sporadic, still do what they can when they can. Indeed, producing the world-famous Glossop Guizers Ancient Pace-Egg Play (of which more later), which they had just invented, they embarked on an ambitious world tour of all the town-centre pubs in Glossop. This is by no means a dry town, so they may well need a year or two to recover. Hopefully they will be back, and very soon too.

Longford Mummers work very hard at what they do. Before now they have had a schedule whereby they visited, in one evening, the following: The Ostrich in Longford, The Holly Bush in Church Broughton, The Rose and Crown in Boylestone, The Shire Horse in Wyaston, The Saracen's Head in Shirley, The Red Lion in Hollington, The Three Horseshoes on Long Lane and back to The Ostrich, presumably for a final and well-earned pint. Or two.

Unlike most Mummers Plays, that are one act, Longford perform the Bampton Mummers Play, which is in two acts, so their schedule is even more gruelling than you'd think at first. Bampton, by the way, is in Oxfordshire, to the east of Cirencester and south-west of Oxford, and is, as you are no doubt well aware, a long way from Derbyshire. However, Bampton have been at it since at least 1847, so they are probably getting used to it now.

Longford started just a bit later - 155 years, to be precise - but they are also very good at it. Also, and this is apparently unusual, some of their mummers are .... (gasp) .... women! There may well be headlines in the Pedants' Weekly, but then, who cares? Well done, them.

Parwich Guizers and Mummers, a lengthy title, but succinct, have been around a goodly while, more than 25 years, and they too perform all around the county at Christmas. Their play started life at Biggin-by-Hartington, certainly well before the 1930s, and a lively spectacle it is too.

The characters, including Beelzebub, who seems to have the main role of getting your money, Bold Slasher the brave soldier, the Quack who brings him back to life and, as you would expect King William, all with blacked-out faces, are very funny, and performed with gusto. Indeed, the sword fight, in which the worthy Sir Knight Slasher cops his whack, is done with as much swashbuckling as Errol Flynn could ever have mustered, but with more convincing accents.

A variation on a theme is produced in Tideswell, or, if you want to sound like you know what you are talking about, Tidza. They have a play called the Tidza Saw Y'eds, which relates the story, true no doubt, of the farmer whose cow gets her head stuck in a gate. The farmer solves the problem by having the cow's head sawn off, as you would, but fear not. Stay your hand from calling the RSPCA, for the Quack comes along and puts everything right by sewing the head back on, and they all live happily ever after. This is the abridged version, you will understand. It would not help if you were blinded by the science of it all.

The characters are The Farmer, The Farmer's Wife (because it is traditional to blame the female of the species), and, of course The Butcher, who performs the dastardly deed. Poor

Old Daisy finishes up pushing up daisies, but the Quack, who is presumably a Quack Vet (although the Royal College of Veterinary Surgeons don't advertise any), performs his miracles, as only Quacks can, and Daisy carries on producing just over three gallons of best moo-juice per diem.

Unlike most of the mumming traditions around the country, Tideswell - sorry, Tidza - have theirs during Wakes Week, the week nearest the 24th of June. Over the hills at Ashover, villagers have staged their mummers production on May Day.

Winster has its guisers, too. Every winter, the Enterer-in does just that, followed by the Black Prince of Paradise, and his dear old Dad, the King of Egypt. Following the traditional sword-fight, the poor prince is snuffed, but the Quack does what Quacks do. Shortly thereafter, Beelzebub comes in, with Little Johnny Jack in hot pursuit, accompanied, as you would expect, by Little Devilly Doubt. Finally, the Horse and Groom come on, and this is the fun bit - the horse is real. Deceased, admittedly, and reduced to a black painted skull with a lower jaw operated by elastic, but equine for all that. The Prince, by the way, is revived by the best way possible - downing, in one, a pint nicked from one of the audience. One assumes that they only do a limited number of shows per night.

How authentic is this? Well, the owner of Winster Hall in about 1870, one Llewellyn Jewitt, had taken photos of many local events, and todays costumes are based entirely on those pictures. How very thoughtful of him.

Mumming? Guizing? Guising? Pace-egging? It matters not a tinker's cuss. If you get the chance, go. Do not delay, do not spend your evenings in your B&B reading stuff like this. It will get you nowhere, and anyway give you only the faintest idea of the tradition at its raucous best. Just keep a hand tightly on your pint.

Derbyshire Passing The Posset

Lady Macbeth, who obviously didn't come from Derbyshire, poisoned one or two unfortunates' possets, and presumably spoilt their weekend.

IN order to be able to Pass the Posset effectively, it is vital that one knows what the Posset is. Extensive research, i.e. I asked my mother-in-law and the postman, who gave me a very old-fashioned look, has shown that of 100% people surveyed, nobody had the first clue what I was on about.

Since I am in the happy position of being the final arbiter on these things, if only for the next few minutes, it is incumbent upon me to enlighten you, so that, should you ever have a posset that needs passing, regardless of in which direction, you will be not only in a position to do so, you will savour the experience.

In fact, it is not only incumbent upon me, it behoves me to do so, which is a phrase that I've always wanted to write, but never had the courage. To be able to use the words posset and behove in one sentence is a rare delight, given to few of us. I take seriously my brief to ensure that you, the reader, do not become de-posseted.

In order for us to find out, you and I, we must travel the county on Christmas Eve. Normally I would be only too happy to drive, but on this occasion, I will let you - I'll explain why later - although I'm perfectly happy to bung you a fiver for the petrol. You see, we must go deep in to Derbyshire, knocking on doors as we go, for passing the posset is more a home-spun custom than one practiced in public. Ask for a posset in the lounge bar of the Rose and Crown, and I suspect that I might know the answer. But, e'er we go, we must discuss what we are looking for. Come hither, whilst I elucidate.

Posset is not the horrible sweet, gooey muck that telly-chefs will have you believe is worth eating, disguised by such strange titles as "Individual Pavlovas with Lemon Posset Cream", for this is a modern phenomenon, and as such, in our search for antiquity, to be ignored. Particularly if served with pulped acai berries, whatever they are, or topped with flaked almonds and candied peel. What we come in search of is altogether more manly, although not so manly that the ladies are excluded.

Whilst a Posset is a vessel, drinking, yeomanry for the use of, posset itself is what is put in a Posset. For posset is a fluid, although sometimes it has so many bits and pieces in it, it is as near as makes no difference solid. With the exception of Pavlova and acai berries, you can put in practically what you want, although only certain things are considered traditional.

Posset, in its original form, was a combination of milk and alcohol - preferably

73

lots of alcohol, so you now see why you are driving. It was certainly so when Shakespeare wrote Macbeth, because Lady Macbeth, who obviously didn't come from Derbyshire, poisoned one or two unfortunates' possets, and presumably spoilt their weekend.

At that time, it was hot milk poured on either sack or ale, sack being a strong sweet wine. Sugar was added, if available, and it was then poured down the waiting neck. QED.

Nowadays, if we should happen to find any posset on our travels (and please drive carefully, the Traditional Yuletide Police will be out looking for the Traditional Yuletide Drunken Motorist) it may well have eggs, treacle, ginger, nutmeg or other spices added to it. In the houses of the more serious drinkers, whisky would be poured in to give it that added zest.

It will be served, we can confidently predict, in a two-handled cup, so that the person on your left can Pass the Posset, and presumably, a whole load of traditional Yuletide germs. Do not worry about them, for the alcohol will kill them before they get anywhere near your tonsils. There are records of oatcake or bread being added, and the resultant mess eaten with a spoon, but this seems a bit like dunking chocolate digestives in your single malt, and thus to be avoided at all costs.

Posset has medicinal qualities, particularly with regard to stomach upsets, which are presumably cured rather than caused. It isn't easy to guess, but after our journey, rest assured that I will tell you. It is also thought to be good for insomnia, which comes as little or no surprise. It must be like pouring half a bottle of gin into your Horlicks, then wondering why you fell asleep in your armchair.

One could argue the validity of such customs, as to whether they are pagan in origin, but it is of no consequence. What matters to you and me, and especially me, since you are looking after your driving licence, is that once again, a Derbyshire tradition revolves around alcohol. When we get back, I promise that I'll let you know if you enjoyed yourself.

Derbyshire Punishments

Gentlemen - well, peasants, then - were cracked over the head with a stick, whilst the females of the species were tickled with a feather on a pole.

LAW and order has long been a bone of contention. On one hand you have those who would like to see the return of the Cat O' Nine Tails for riding a bicycle without a bell, whilst others would be a bit more liberal, and feel that no crime is so serious that it can't be remedied by a short period on the Naughty Step.

Because there has always been such a disparity, the punishment has rarely been decided by one person, with the exception being the Royal Navy, where things were particularly brutal. It seems odd that there was a system that could cripple a man for life, when there was a shortage of trained seamen, because of a relatively minor misdemeanour.

We are going to look at some of the punishments that were traditionally used throughout the county, although few were exclusive to Derbyshire. You just get the impression that the people we are talking about seemed to enjoy the spectacle more. We will not go in to any great depth, for it may well have dawned in upon you by now that this is not within our purview, and there are serious historians, theologians and scholars better qualified than your current pen-monger, who will produce big fat books with hard covers, costing the Gross National Debt of several eastern European states, and couched in terms that few if any can understand. Most of these books finish up in second-hand bookshops, and are bought to cure a wonky piano leg.

Riding the Stang is just about dead these days, but, as far as can be determined, it involved a sort of Trial by Ridicule. Nowadays, there are innumerable reality television shows, quizzes and competitions that do exactly the same thing, without the need for having beaten your wife. However, if you had done just that, the wittiest man in the village was put aboard a ladder, armed with a key or stick, and in the other hand a dripping-pan, and carried at shoulder height through the community. The ladder was known as a Stang.

Everybody else in the village joins in, with tin cans, horns, trumpets, a euphonium if you happen to have one lying about the house, indeed, anything that can make a discordant noise. North of the border, there are bagpipes.

The procession travels through the village, stopping every few yards for a scurrilous poem about the miscreant to be be recited very loudly, which would have modern lawyers specialising in slander jumping up and down, with £ signs in their eyes.

In the more extreme cases, usually involving marital infidelity, effigies were paraded through the streets. This was done to the full, carried out over three days, and several times each day, stopping outside the house of the "defendant", as we currently call him. If it was a

We all know about being put in the stocks. If nothing else, it was a way for the villagers to make use of any rotting vegetation

particularly serious case, then the effigies were burned, usually outside the home of the malefactor. The last recorded place for this to happen in these 'ere parts was at Haddon, but no date is recorded. There are also cases of the accused being forced to ride atop the ladder.

Those who fell asleep in church, and there can be no better place after a hard week to have a swift nap on the Sabbath, were dealt with summarily, and in a terribly sexist way. Enter, Stage Left, the Sluggard Waker. Gentlemen - well, peasants, then - were cracked over the head with a stick, whilst the females of the species were tickled with a feather on a pole. Apparently.

We all know about being put in the stocks. If nothing else, it was a way for the villagers to make use of any rotting vegetation, iffy eggs or other slops that were lying around the house, and which these days find their way to the back of the fridge, behind a pot of hazelnut yoghurt that was out of date last half-term. They were, purely and simply, used as ammunition, and, we have it on the greatest authority, were far more effective than the average ASBO. Slimy Brussels sprouts at ten paces are a fiercesome prospect.

These were perhaps the most common punishments, bar for two others, these being the Ducking Stool and the Scold's Bridle.

The Scold's Bridle was a method whereby a metal frame, not dissimilar to a rugby players scrum-cap, but with a tongue depressor, were put over over a nagging wife's head, and locked in place. The truly professional nag would have a tongue strong enough to bend even the finest steel, and anyway, for it to happen, you would have to admit in public that the old girl had been giving you GBH of the ear-hole. This is not good for one's credibility, so it was rarely invoked.

More common was the Ducking Stool, whereby a woman who did something wrong, such as burning your porridge, mentioning that you'd just trodden half a ton of pigs' doings through the house, or anything else that the lads had decided over a pint at the local was a bit off, was sentenced to be ducked.

It was, to be fair, most commonly used for the Nag (see above), but you weren't going to admit to that in front of all the blokes down at The Red Lion, so any trumped-up charge would suffice. The poor wife, at the centre of a huge scrum, would be taken to the local pond, where a chair on a pivot was waiting.

In the less well regulated communities, it was a permanent feature, bearing in mind that there were no courts then, and the landlord usually had a casting vote. She was strapped in to said chair and given the opportunity to assess the temperature of the water, until she foreswore to mend her evil ways, whatever they were.

There are moves to have this system reintroduced, and if you wish to support.... (Publisher's Note: At this point the publisher's wife and the author's wife conversed, and it was decided nem con that if this paragraph were continued, the publisher and the author would have ample opportunity to discuss things further from the safety and comfort of their hospital beds, once somebody had replaced the teeth they lost in the earlier discussions. Thank You).

There is nothing more to say about traditional punishments.

Eyam & The Plague

Thou canst not, as yette, buy little plastycke coffins with ye nayme Eyam thereuponne, or stick-onne sores, but itte is onlie a matter of tyme.

ONNE ye seconde daye of Septembre, in ye yeare of Grace 1665, didst Ye Plague make an deadly visytation uponne ye vyllage of Eyam, in Darbyshire, and thereby hangeth a tale.

Legende hath it thatte ye vyllagers didst isolate themselves, atte ye worde of ye Vicar, ye Reverend Williame Mompesson, butte sadlie this is probablie only halfe true, at bestte. Ye reverend gentlemanne was a goode and saintlie manne, and did make sure that ye people of ye vyllage stayed putte, so thatte Ye Plage spreadeth not, but not befoure he hadst gotte his owne kiddes out of ye place, to a safe haven. To her eternal creditte did ye Mistresse Mompesson stay, and verily didst she paye with her lyfe. If anyone be ye hero of ye piece it be her, for her goode and saintlie husband hadde asked her to go, but she refuseth.

Tis said that ye vyllagers did stay in ye boundaries of their own communittye, butte this be a falsehoode and a foul calumnie. There be a cayse on recorde of a woman fromme Eyam that wandereth yea to Tideswell, and was requested to get herselffe hence, by the simple means of stoning herre. This be simplie meane. It be probable that others did similar stuntes pulle.

Ye vyllage was fed by ye people of nearby Sheffielde, who bringeth foode and placeth it nearbye whatte be now knowne as Mompesson's Well. Ye paymente was made with coines of ye realme, left in vinegar, for to stop the Plague from spreading. Ye vyllagers goeth not beyond this poynte, but onlye because ye good burghers of Sheffielde spake Thus.

"Nah den, dee, if dah teks one step more, astle fill dee full o' lead from dis 'ere musket, an' dah'll see worra good shotte ah am. Does da see worra meean?"

For thys reasone are ye men of Sheffielde respectfullie known as "Dee-dahs" to ye men of Darbyshire, even unto this verye daye.

Many are knowne to have leffte ye vyllage, and encamped even in tentes in ye surroundynge countriesyde, so it seemeth prettie lykelie that ye stories of all ye good men and wimmin of Eyam staying there, and making ye supreme sacrifyce, over-eggeth ye puddinge. Humanne nature is oft an uglie manifestationne.

Ye Plague left ye vyllage in ye yere of Our Lord 1666, onne ye firste daye of Novembyre. It left a vyllage devastated, but rype for manie to make claims that, e'en now, are believed by manye, although ye scholars are uncoverryng ye truthe, and even ye museume in Eyam sayeth that half of it was rubbyshe. Let it not detract, though, from ye lion-lyke courrage of manye of ye populayse, who didst surrender their verye lives, to ye number of anything fromme 260 to 370. Ye populayse of ye vyllage was onlie 260, or 800, dependantte uponne whom thous lysteneth to, and Ye Visitation leaveth butte 83, or 430. One wondereth who to believeth. It mattereth notte, for it leaveth a scant quarter of ye menne and wymmin. Ye devastation of ye Plague and ye stories surroundynge itte are celebrated eache yere in ye Vyllage, with ye gyvinge of thankes, althoughe fore whatte is hard to understande.

Ye Plague is not of itselfe a traditionne, but ye making of much mileage with mythes and legendes is, with ye selling of Post Cardes, gyded toures shewing where ye people did expire, repulsyve wax models of ye dying, displayinge manie a buboe and oft, and generalle ghoulishnesse. There be Plague Plaques throughout ye townshippe, that showeth where the many dyed, and ye touristtes do come and pointte, and laugh immoderatelie, for ye Plague is no more. Thou canst not, as yette, buy little plastycke coffins with ye nayme Eyam thereuponne, or stick-onne sores, but itte is onlie a matter of tyme.

Flagg Races

It goes without saying that there is a certain element of risk, and in the event of, say, a broken leg, there is often the sad spectacle of a shooting, but then, jockeys are expendable.

IT was the best of times, it was the worst of times, and not only because it was the year that Manfred von Richthofen, better known as the Red Baron, and JRR Tolkein were born. It also depended upon the number of legs you have, because for all the endless witterings of evolutionists against creationists, there is no animal with three legs.

Think how useful it would be. You could drive your car easier, since you'd have a foot ready over each pedal, you could only ever be out LBW in cricket, largely because there would be a leg in front of each stump, and you would never need to buy a shooting stick. If one leg got tired, you'd still have the other two to stand on, so such things as verrucas and in-growing toenails would be only half the worry. Of course, your tailor would need to be pretty talented, and your bill at Wynsor's House of Shoes would go up a bit, but it seems a small price to pay.

However, riding a horse would, without doubt, be a problem. Which brings us back neatly to 1892, when Flagg Races were first held.

Imagine, if you will, the year 1903. Richthofen and Tolkein are sitting in a Hamburg pub, accompanied by their exact contemporaries, actresses Margaret Rutherford and Mary Pickford, car maker Gaston Chevrolet and Emperor Haile Selassie. They are all discussing what they will do for a joint twenty-first birthday party. Huge gatherings of glitterati have been mooted, oceans of caviare, Ferrero Rocher chockies being borne hither and yon by perspiring flunkies, the candlelight winking on the chandeliers, fawning acquaintances, attempting to curry favour, bring ever more outlandish gifts. The air would be full of the tinkling laughter of the social elite, the heady scent of Champagne, the lingering odour of the photographers' magnesium flares.

"Nah, tell you what," said Miss Pickford, "I got a better idea, me. What if we got into one of Gastie's horseless carriages, and went up to the coldest, wettest, windiest part of Derbyshire, and watched all the loonies racing at Flagg? We could have hot-dogs, or burgers, or soggy chips. All this posh stuff gives me the burps."

" 'Ere, no, what abaht this, then? 'Stead of messing about in cars, we could go in one of Manfred's aeroplanes, that'd be, like, way cool!" murmured Tolkein.

"Zis is not ze possible being, da wir kein airfield having are, and it impossible is, ze aeroplane zu landen, wizout ze smooth piece of grass. Ve must vait until ze helikopter invented is."

"Oh, I say," said Gaston, for despite his name he was acutely aware of being American, and wanted to hide the fact, "This all sounds terribly jolly, what, absolutely bang on and all that, but what exactly happens? How does a chap race a flag? Sounds jolly complicated, what?"

"Quite," said Miss Rutherford, draining the last of the litre of Pilsener from the bottom of her Stein. She stubbed her cigar out, thoughtfully, belched delicately into her tiny, embroidered silk handkerchief, and looked quizzically around the schnapps-stained table. "One is dying to know."

"Gordon Bennet!" exclaimed Haile Selassie, "Don't you lot know nothing? It's simple."

Fortunately, the wise and the powerful have ever wanted their bon mots to be remembered for eternity and so, tape recorders not having been invented, there were three stenographers and two secretaries present, to make sure that every pearl of wisdom that might be dropped would last for eons, or at least until the newspapers corrupted it beyond all recognition. This, roughly, is a transcript of what was said.

The term Steeplechase derives from when horse races went from one church steeple to the next, by whichever route the riders chose, usually the most direct. Admittedly, a detour down the A515 is smoother, and takes in less jumps, but there's often a traffic queue at the Bull i't Thorn pub, and it can take ages. Just to be awkward, Flagg church doesn't have a steeple, so they had to call it a point-to-point, which doesn't have that same class about it, never mind that now the churches don't get a look-in, the vicar has to be a bit careful about being seen at Honest Joe's betting stall.

The horses race on a circuit between the villages of Flagg and Pomeroy, over open country. Now, one of the features of open country, particularly in Derbyshire, is that there are hundreds of dry stone walls, which, if you wish to win the race, you have to jump over, preferably whilst still on your horse. It goes without saying that there is a certain element of risk, and in the event of, say, a broken leg, there is often the sad spectacle of a shooting, but then, jockeys are expendable.

The main worry is if the horse gets injured, and animal welfare activists will make much noise about this. It is worth remembering that a little, nine-stone man is sat upon a huge great animal that weighs up to about 1,300lb, or, if you prefer, 92st 12lb. If that 92st 12lb decides that it doesn't fancy jumping over a pile of stones, there is very little that the 9st 4oz on its back is going to be able to do about it, other than hang on as tight as he can. If he doesn't, falling 16 hands doesn't sound too bad, but there is a formula. Convert that into five feet, the distance from saddle to floor, add height of jockey, because he sure as eggs isn't going to fall backside first, multiply by the speed of the horse, add the kinetic weight of being dragged by one foot in a stirrup, divide by the number of legs on the horse, since only one is likely to kick you, add the length of the parabola you will prescribe in mid-air, divide by 2 x Pi x r, and divide by the indignity of the crowds laughing at you. Adding the number you first thought of is optional. This, we are assured by veterinary experts, means that the horse will win the argument, without fail.

Ask a horse if it will mind taking part in a race, especially with the risk to wind, limb and hoof, and it will make the above calculation, factoring in that it is Easter Tuesday, and the rider will be full of chocolate plus other festive excesses, and it will, almost exclusively, say "Neigh!". Horses do not mind, for horses are no fools.

There is something which says that trying to get a horse to do what it doesn't want to is the personification of stupidity, but that is a matter between man and beast. By the same token, the average nag, being covered in furry stuff, doesn't mind being 1,000ft above sea level, where every schoolboy knows that the temperature is 3.33 degress (F) lower. There is also no escaping the fact that the weather at Easter is unpredictable. Races have been held in rain, hail, sleet, snow, fog and blazing sunshine, sometimes on the same afternoon.

Once upon a time, in the sweet lang syne, there were many such horse races across the country, but Flagg is the last of them. You could argue that Derbyshire is behind the times, that they haven't moved on from when the village was recorded as 'Flagun' in the Domesday book, but the more plausible argument is that ancient customs are often worth preserving. In fact, you can bet on it!

One of the features of open country, particularly in Derbyshire, is that there are hundreds of dry stone walls

Grindon Hedgehog Rolling

Hedgehogs turn into a perfect sphere and Mrs Tiggywinkle could feel herself rotating laterally, then longitudinally, and then all over the place.

NOT many of us can have got through life without rolling down a hillside. Possibly, there may be a few odd individuals from the fenlands of Cambridgeshire, who never took a holiday, and have thus never seen a hill, but there can't be many.

Most of us, as children, must have lain down at the top of a grassy bank, tucked our arms in and rolled to the bottom, or as near as the parabola that the rolling human prescribes makes possible.

Indeed, looking out the window as I write, there is a verdant slope, down which my own children have rolled many a time and oft, as has my wife, although rather more recently than is perhaps wise. Inevitably, the grandchildren wanted to have a go, but it took someone to show them, and grandparents do not need to maintain the air of gravitas that parents do. I have reached the stage of portliness that late middle age brings in the male of the species, and would probably have merely rocked myself to sleep, but my spouse has succumbed somewhat less to the ravages of time, and was first in the queue to get extremely dizzy, whilst the world went green/blue/green/blue/green/blue for a few terrifying seconds.

I dread to think what may have been deposited on that grass over the past few years, but diplomacy dictates that one keeps such thoughts to oneself. The grandchildren bravely followed suit.

In some places, it is traditional to roll cheeses down hillsides, and then go after them, which seems a bit odd. Surely, it would be easier to cut a few bits off the cheese, thus making it rectangular, as well as providing necessary sustenance for the afternoon's rigours. The cheese would not roll as far, there would be less chance of injury or becoming besmirched with sheeps doings, and you could get to your supper that much more quickly. However, the good burghers of Cooper's Hill, deep in the Cotswolds near Gloucester, insist on doing this, and annually at that, although it is only a matter of time before Nanny State steps in, and insists on parachutes, or speed limits, or compulsory rest periods.

Derbyshire is not necessarily noted for the rolling of cheeses, if only because Sage Derby is a bit on the soft side, and the hills around Buxton are sufficiently lethal and rocky that rolling Buxton Blue cheeses down them palls somewhat, but the county is not left behind. In the rolling stakes, though, all that is left to roll, that is locally available, is hedgehogs.

Before you jump on to your high horse, calling evil down upon those who harm hedgehogs, their heirs and assigns, and muttering imprecations concerning our love for wildlife, let me assure you that no hedgehogs were harmed in the writing of this article. Let me explain.

On a warm, summer's day on a hill above the village of Grindon, which may or may not be in Derbyshire, depending upon who you are talking to, Mrs Tiggywinkle strolled out of her tiny little cottage, with a tiny little bag of the day's washing and a tiny little bag of pegs in her tiny little front paws. She ambled across the grass, a tiny little hedgehog tune on her tiny little lips, when a large and grubby hand picked her up.

Straight away, for she had been trained by her father, who had been a hedgehog in the SAS (Special Animal Service), she rolled into a tight little ball and waited for what might come next. She felt herself swing backwards, and then she felt herself swing forwards, then backwards again, followed by a strange feeling of weightlessness. All she could hear was the rushing of the wind, then she hit the ground with a spike-bending thud, and felt herself begin to roll, at speed.

Unlike humans, who make a pretty untidy ball, and thus roll sideways, hedgehogs turn into a perfect sphere, and Mrs Tiggywinkle could feel herself rotating laterally, then longitudinally, and then all over the place. She uttered a particularly unladylike, hedgehog expression, that her father had also taught her, during one of his less lucid moments after an acorn-cup full of what had leaked from a potato, and turned out be practically neat vodka. Ladies using such language, during the 19th century, was almost unheard of, but since Mrs Tiggywinkle was so tightly rolled up, it was completely unheard, except by one or two fleas who were too shocked to worry unduly.

She rolled to a halt, covered in leaves, twigs, petals and sticky stuff, looking like those pictures you see of the Paras, on the telly, only this was 63 years before the TV would be invented. After a short while, to ascertain it was safe, she slowly uncurled, looking carefully around for the dastardly mitt that had perpetrated this evil. Nobody was in sight, which was hardly surprising, for she had travelled some considerable distance, courtesy of Sir Isaac Newton. She gazed up at the hill, which she knew was the only route back home.

"Cor, I ain't half dizzy," she said to herself. "I dunno if I'm in Staffordshire or Derbyshire, I come that far."

Slowly, she trudged up the hill, to sort out her washing. The child that had spoiled her afternoon went home and told his sister, who told her mum, who told her husband, and little Jimmy was put over a knee and given a workmanlike hiding for cruelty to animals. Jimmy, as he gazed at the floor, and his father's boots, and heard the swish of the descending hand, was far more bothered about cruelty to humans, and one in particular.

Many years later, he told his own son about what had happened that fateful summer's day, and Jimmy's son told his son, and the grandson told his son, for there was little to do in Grindon, in those days. This is now a tradition.

However, Grindon, still not knowing whether it was in Staffordshire or Derbyshire, developed a love for the hedgehog, and when they heard about the sport of Hedgehog Rolling currently sweeping across the Southern United States, unlike China where the hedgehog is sacred, they were horrified.

In order to make the terrible plight of the hedgehog known across the globe, they resurrected Hedgehog Rolling at their annual well-dressing, which is, no matter how you may argue geography, a Derbyshire custom. The difference is, the hedgehogs are not real, for those who roll them are sometimes a little too long in the tooth for a smacked bottom, and are better qualified as smacker than smackee. Instead, the animals are made out of cones, and twigs, and painted up to look realistic.

And before you say that this is not exactly an ancient custom, remember, the twigs that the modern hedgehog is made from are descended from the very ones that Mrs Tiggywinkle rolled through, all those years ago. History repeats itself again!

In order to make the terrible plight of the hedgehog known across the globe, Hedgehog Rolling was introduced at a well-dressing festival

Hayfield May Queen

You wouldn't want a May Queen with bunions. She can hardly wear a pair of Army boots with the old royal gown, now, can she?

THE longest standing continual procession of its kind in the country. Now, that is not the sort of statement that you would want to take issue with, and for several reasons. Firstly, if it is true, and you argued, the May Queen would doubtless, and justifiably, belt you one with her sceptre. Secondly, it would be nice to think it is true, because it has style. Thirdly, there is no evidence to gainsay it, and frankly, if there were, it would be best kept to oneself. It would not do for a town outside of Derbyshire to claim the title. And anyway, you can look in vain, you won't find another May Queen Procession which has been going, unbroken, since 1928 - and that was a revival!

The May Queen is elected each year, unlike our Monarch, who, despite the underhand dealings of various Republican ratbags of the worst sort, does not need to be. Not that the vast majority of us could care less one way or the other, it's just that you'd be left with a problem of who to put on the stamps. Nothing could be worse than licking the back of the Prime Minister's head. So, a suitable young lady is named as May Queen, and at the same time (I hope I've got this right, that sceptre looks heavy), the Princess and Rosebud are chosen.

As far as can be ascertained, the Queen - Hayfield's, that is - is not asked to meet with politicians (which must be a relief), open a new Sainsbury's or go to Ascot and meet hordes of fawning commoners like what we are.

However, in one respect, she actually has a distinct advantage over our own dear Sovereign, in that she gets a procession second to none. No Guardsmen on horseback, no thousands of stony-faced coppers lining the route, no standing on the balcony at Buck House, waving, when the poor woman just wants to get inside, kick her shoes off and get at the sandwiches.

The May Queen is followed by the Petal Girls, the Princess, Rosebud, the Beefeaters, the Sword and Shield Bearers, any visiting Queens there may happen to be, brass bands, pipe bands, dancing troupes and a multitude of minions, acolytes, hangers-on and the hoi-polloi.

She has to look pleased to be there, as indeed does any queen, and she has to have a convincing royal wave. The whole procession is done on foot. The cavalcade starts at the top end of the village, near what is called the May Queen Field, just off Swallowhouse Lane, goes through the entire length of the village on one side, crosses the main A624, and then goes through the remainder.

It used to go all the way to Birch Vale, but it is a long way, and you wouldn't want a May

Queen with bunions. She can hardly wear a pair of Army boots with the old royal gown, now, can she?

She isn't finished, because she now has to go all the way back to the May Queen Field, where she is eventually crowned. Each year, the procession is led by the outgoing Queen, with the Queen Elect bringing up the rear. It is a wonderful excuse to get all the children in the village doing something and it attracts a procession of 500 to 600 people. The Queen, who is usually in her mid to late teens, is then a local celebrity for the year, taking part in all manner of village events, as she wishes. Unlike our Sovereign, she can pick and choose, without some civil servant sticking his beak in.

Originally, the parade was not just for fun, but was a major event for the Saturday Fund, which provided health care in the days before the National Health Service. Such a thing has not been needed since 1948, since it wouldn't make much of a dent in the NHS's annual budget of £100 million-or-so. Nowadays the money raised is used for other good causes.

There's also a fell run called the Hayfield May Queen, which is run in the same week as the carnival parade. Various people who are disgustingly fit, and have bulging muscles in places where most of us didn't even know we had places, leg it half way round the county, going up hill and down dale, and get back all sweaty and out of breath, prior to being given a prize. They are, of course, completely insane, and thoroughly deserving of the applause that the crowd so readily give them. Just thinking about it makes some of us go weak at the knees, and in need of a lie-down and a cup of tea.

Finally, Hayfield has one of the best pub names in the entire world. It is called the Lantern Pike, named after a nearby hill, which was more than probably a beacon, before somebody invented Morse Code and radios. It has nothing to do with it, but it still conjures up images of nefarious activities, smuggling, highwaymen or dark goings-on in the middle of the night, with shadowy figures, carrying a swinging lantern on the end of a pikestaff, and with a brace of pistols at the ready. They be the Royalists, brave hardy men - the men that defend the Queen. Any Queen.

Longshaw Sheepdog Trials

The poor old dog, who is probably just dying to sink a fang or two into the stroppy, woolly things, isn't allowed to, on pain of disqualification.

WERE you to ask most folk what they think the biggest influence Wales has had on Derbyshire, there are several answers you might get.
The Welsh are famous for mining, although there are, at the time of writing, no deep mines left. Derbyshire also had hundreds of mines, so the connection is obvious. Sorry. Nil Pointe. Keine Puenkte.
There are a few connections, the main one being the use of Tredegar Rings, the steel formers that replaced pit props, and were thought to be much safer, but that is about it. What about if you want to get to Wales, and you live in Sheffield? Well, true enough, it's quite handy to go via Ashford-in-the-Water, Taddington, Brierlow Bar, Harpur Hill and on to the A53 to Leek, but it probably hasn't changed the culture of either county much.
The influence was to do with a trial, in 1873. Ha! Criminality, you exclaim, and quite justifiably, we all know that Taffy was a Welshman, Taffy was a Thief, he come round my gaff and half-inched a piece of beef. But, once again, no.
Wales has its own breed of cattle called the Welsh Black and there is no finer meat to eat at a banquet celebrating Wales beating England at Twickenham. Or Cardiff. However, we digress.
The trial was held at Y Bala, which most people just know as Bala, if only because of Bala Lake, which isn't. Isn't Bala Lake, I mean, it is Llyn Tegid, and is famous for having a unique breed of fish, the gwyniad, a type of salmon. However we digress again. The trial we refer to was the very first recorded Sheepdog Trial. And before we go any further it is important that we get the old joke out of the way that says they were all found guilty. Thank You.
Derbyshire has quite a few Sheepdog Trials, the best known perhaps being Bamford, Dovedale, Hope, Hayfield and Longshaw. Longshaw, indeed, is the longest running such event in England, starting in 1898, so it's a fair bet that, since the Welsh had been at it from 1873, only Welshmen won it for the first 25 years. Quite right, too. However, we digress.
The only things that have interfered with the Longshaw trials were two world wars, and it is an extremely popular event by any standards. To be fair, this is about the only sport in the world where the dog is smarter than man, which is a humbling experience, but also the only one that could have a trophy called the Derbyshire Times Driving Crook, and keep a straight face.

Whilst Longshaw, in the north of the county, is the home of the oldest trials in England, there are others scattered around

Mind you, it's a good bet that the face which won - the human one, that is - might not be too straight that evening in the Fox House Inn, which is just over the road. Their Steak and Ale Pie is excellent, as is the bitter beer. The things one has to do for research.

As most of us have seen on "One Man And His Dog", the dogs are put through various tests which they have to perform despite some bloke in a cloth cap whistling at him all the time.

It must be terribly hard to concentrate. To put the popularity of the sport in to perspective, "One Man..." attracted audiences of eight million, and it isn't hard to see why. We are, at heart, a rural creature, despite the fact that so many now live in urban sprawl.

Each dog has to go through the Cast, or being sent off, the Lift, which is actually rounding the sheep up, the Bring which is self-explanatory, and then things get difficult.

The next bit is the Away Drive, which goes contrary to the dog's nature, since it doesn't want to move sheep away from the shepherd, so there is some teamwork involved.

After that comes the Cross Drive, then the Shed, where one or two sheep are separated from the remainder and finally the Pen, which is the very last place the sheep have to go, and the very last place that they want to go. The poor old dog, who is probably just dying to sink a fang or two into the stroppy, woolly things, isn't allowed to, on pain of disqualification.

The most common dog used at any sheepdog trial is the Border Collie, although there are purists who will tell you that it was the Welsh Border, and since trialling is older in Wales, it is a Welsh Collie. However, we digress.

Yet more surprisingly, there are competitors from all over the world. Indeed, if you think of the dog we now know as the German Shepherd (and why isn't it German Sheepdog?), it shows that using dogs to herd animals isn't a British invention. Or a Welsh one, even, but we digress. Perhaps the most famous, certainly of the British Border Collies was Shep, who millions of Blue Peter fans will remember as John Noakes' permanent companion ("And here we are on the end of a parachute at 40,000 feet... Get Down, Shep!") Who could forget?

Of course, Lassie was a Collie, but not a Border Collie, and when you think that the first Lassie film was in 1943, and the last in 2005, it would have taken a remarkable mutt to have played the lead in all of them. Lassie (female) has been played by Pal, Baby, Mire, Hey Hey, Boy, Howard, Mason and Rockie (all male). There was never a film called Lassie Rounds Up Sheep, or Lassie On Trial, which is a great shame. There could be some mileage in that. Lassie was also never Welsh, but we digress.

As well as the regional sheepdog trials, there are international events, although the name is slightly confusing. These are only between the four home nations. By one of those strange quirks of fate, at a recent such event, the English entry in the Young Handler class was one Megan Jenkins, which sounds just a bit un-English to some. However, we digress.

There are also world events, which rather prompts such questions as "What is the Swedish for 'Come-Bye'." I know only that the French, if they want their hound to sit, they do not say "Asseyez Vous", but go for the simpler "Seet!"

Whilst Longshaw, in the north of the county, is the home of the oldest trials in England, there are others scattered around. Hayfield in the west, Bamford which is actually a fraction further north than Longshaw, but further west, Dovedale which is a bit to the south, and Hope which isn't that far from Bamford. Truth to tell, it wouldn't be too far to drive your sheep, assuming that you have any. That isn't likely, mind, because if you did, you'd know all this stuff anyway, so you'd be wasting your time which could be better employed training your dogs. However, we digress.

If you have ever watched "One Man and His Dog", you will realise that we will never hear the dulcet tones of Phil Drabble again, but if you wish to relive the pleasures, and get massive quantities of fresh air at the same time, get yourself to a sheepdog trial. They are all posted on the Internet, and there are always directions as to how to get there. Follow them carefully, and whatever you do, do not digress.

Matlock Bath Venetian Nights

It is an extremely colourful spectacle, well worth going out, trying to find a parking space, walking miles and getting rained on for.

THE next time that you are stuck in a massive traffic jam in Matlock Bath, surrounded by a plethora of Harley Davidsons, Hondas, Suzukis, Kawasakis and the odd Triumph, take heart. All is not lost.

You may well be breathing almost pure diesel fumes from the bus just in front of you that hasn't moved for 40 minutes, with a bored driver reading the paper, but you still have a link with ancient Venice. Not that Matlock Bath was ever the first city of a republic, as Venice was, and as far as is known, Derbyshire was never invaded by Napoleon, although it was a close run thing. In 1797, when Monsieur Bonaparte was quaffing the congratulatory champagne in Italy, various others who had an allegiance to him were busy attempting to invade Britain, in the tiny Welsh fishing village of Fishguard. Having said that, it isn't tiny now, and anyway, the Welsh call it Abergwaun.

Nevertheless, here it was that 1,400 Frenchmen landed, and were met by "troops of the line to the number of several thousand". Actually, there weren't any troops there; what there was seems to have been many local Welshwomen, in traditional red cloaks and tall black hats, getting upset and rounding up Johnny Frenchman with pitchforks and the like. This is not an indictment on the appearance of Welsh womanhood. The Surrender was signed in a local pub, Y Dderwen Frenhinol (The Royal Oak), which still contains some artefacts, including a French musket, looking as though it were captured yesterday.

The other connection with Venice, which is worth considering as your engine slowly overheats, is that Venice has been declared a No-Car Zone. Surprised? No. Nor me.

It was around this time that those who normally went on the Grand Tour of Europe were beginning to realise that it was a tad risky, what with heads rolling all over the place, and revolutionary zeal being the order of the day. They had to look closer afield, if there is such a phrase, and Matlock was the obvious choice. After all, it had already been compared with Alpine Switzerland by Lord Byron, and who are we to argue? There had been Royal visitors, too, although not until 1832, when the young Princess Victoria graced the town with her regal presence, and then later, when Queen, in 1844. And this, best beloved, is when it all begins.

When Princess Victoria first came to Matlock Bath, she was enchanted with the light of candles reflecting in the waters of the River Derwent, presumably as poor, innocent lead miners wandered their way to work in the pitch dark, using the only light-source available. In 1897, somebody remembered this, which is pretty convenient, and light bulbs began to come on, albeit figuratively.

You see, this was the year of Queen Victoria's Diamond Jubilee, and if the local dignitaries wanted to be in with a shout for an honour or two, the odd knighthood, maybe, or membership of the Victorian Order, something had to be done, which would not only have to get back to Her Majesty, but that would presumably amuse her as well. There are those who will sell their birthright for a mess of letters after their name. What better way than reminding the Queen of her childhood, and without the expense of dirty great big statues that all look remarkably similar. Bronze wasn't cheap in the 19th century. With the value of hindsight, it might have been better to make all those likenesses when Her Majesty was a bit younger, and therefore a tad slimmer. Think of the metal you could have saved.

Anyway, the good people of the Derwent Gorge went one better, and instead of wasting vast quantities of molten metal, celebrated the Diamond Jubilee by building a whole load of boats, obviously working on the principle that bronze is not one of those things that floats very well. In the very first show, there were processions with "fairy lamps, Chinese and Japanese lanterns, a torchlight procession and the rockfaces lit by coloured bonfires", which sounds a bit like Guy Fawkes night on amphetamines. Doubtless, some kind sycophant sent photographs of all this to the Queen, who equally doubtlessly turned to the nearest equerry with the immortal quote: "When are they going to invent colour photography?"

Of course, all this would have died a natural death, were it not for the invention of the railways. Once the Midland, still commemorated by a local hotel, built a line to Matlock, the peasantry flocked there, to enjoy what had previously only been the province of the more genteel. The more genteel promptly went elsewhere, leaving the way open for the likes of us.

The other invention that bucked things up a bit was electricity. It is a sight easier to build a boat with electric lights, although I should imagine you need a very long wire from the nearest plug hole. I am no expert.

Nowadays, many boats take part in the cavalcade, disguised in a myriad different ways, and it is an extremely colourful spectacle. Indeed, dare I say, it is well worth going out, trying to find a parking space, walking miles and getting rained on for. Perhaps the piece de resistance, though, is the fact that there is still one boat decorated with candles, in the Victorian style. This is also as a result of letters after names, for somebody with the cipher MMBVBBA after his moniker must have suggested it. Whether this was for reasons of sucking up to a late monarch, or in the name of traditionalism, is unknown, but it is a singular privilege to be a Member of the Matlock Bath Venetian Boat Builders' Association. So much so, in fact, that in 1903, the event was recognised by no less a personage than Sir Richard Arkwright, in whose name there is a shocking boat-connected pun which we will pass over, who presented a Cup, to be competed for. It is called, as you might imagine, the Arkwright Cup.

As well as the boats being decorated, there are also illuminations on the river banks, with all manner of moving imagery. As you walk along, between street lamps, suddenly a 6ft green frog materialises out of nowhere, or at least, out of cables that you can't see in the dark, and you get the shock of your life. As it were.

Blondins cross rivers, aeroplanes fly silently through the night, coaches bearing Cinderellas travel their short, electrical journey ad infinitum and later, fireworks light the sky. It is traditional to go "Ooh" or "Aah" in all the right places, and so you should, for it is an impressive display, especially within the confines of the narrow valley.

If you are not yet convinced, let us consider another point. A trip to Venice, the City of Light, is going to set you back quite a bit of folding money, whereas Matlock Bath is but a short drive from most parts of the country - of course, if you have bought this in Britain, and are currently reading it in Melbourne, or Dallas, this won't help much.

You will not need to spend hours in some grotty departure lounge, getting a back-ache on peeling plastic chairs that were modern when aeroplanes still had propellers. You will not need to put up with airline catering, which consists of different coloured plastics on a plastic plate covered with plastic. The cling-film is generally the most nutritious part. You will not need to stand in Baggage Reclaim, to find out that your underwear is currently in Buenos Aires. You will not need to get ripped off by taxi drivers in those places where the roads are not 99% water, driving 17 miles then dropping you off at your hotel, which is 500 yards from the airport, and where you spend most of the night listening to the flaps coming down on aircraft about 9in above your head, prior to the screech of tortured rubber as they hit the Italian landscape.

This saving in time and money can then be wisely invested. Now that the genteel have gone elsewhere, there are plenty of chip shops to choose from, and if you are missing the feel of Italy, some even do pizza. One of them, where you can sit at tables on the pavement, if it isn't raining, does a mean spaghetti bolognese with a halfway decent Chianti. You won't know the difference.

Pikehall Harness Racing

A cob is a breed of horse in some places, but in Derbyshire it means what Sheffield folk would call a breadcake.

IT reads like one of the more lurid Paperback Romances. You know the ones, with half-clad females pouting on the front cover, often holding a glass of Champagne, or even a cigarette holder, although you haven't seen one being used for real in over 20 years.

They're the sort of books where the hero is never called Nigel or Brian, but Brent, or Rock, or Guy. Poor old Norman never gets a look in, particularly on page eight, where the heroine is freely distributing her favours to all and sundry, except Norman, who is still playing whist in the drawing room with Keith.

Nobody ever drives a Fiesta or drinks pints, nobody does their shopping at Marks and Sparks, they are all too busy swanning around Harrods in dodgy shoes from Prada, with eleven-inch heels. The gentlemen, for you don't find normal blokes, get their suits from Gieves and Hawkes, rather than Burtons, and their shoes (doubtless Derbys or Oxfords) from a little chap they know on Cathedral Close. Never, in all the history of Mills and Boon, have you seen a pair of smelly old trainers that somebody picked up on the market for nine quid, with a free pair of Odor-Eaters.

Therefore, one was a tad suspicious when one read that Levi Joe and his New York Sweetheart had not only been seen apart, but there was Another Man. It appears that his Premier Dream was to have a word with Sir Bobby (not that one, one trusts), and sort out about Elizabeth Ann and her Little Legs. That, it seems, would have made her some kind of Magical Star, and then he could do something about her addiction to Pantihistamine. I may have got the story mixed up, you know what it's like on a foggy day, and the old ear-holes ain't what they used to be.

Where did one hear these scurrilous whispers? In the City? The Gossip Desk of the Weekly Blackmail including Celebrity Slur? At a cocktail party, when one was invited to one of the many Stately Homes around here? No, not quite. It was in a tiny little hamlet called Pikehall, just off the A5102, where many go, just to see the nearby Gotham Curve, the tightest bend on the National Railway Network. For the connoisseur, it has a radius of two-and-a-half chains, which, in layman's terms, means that if the choo-choo goes too fast, it falls off the rails, which is not approved.

In amongst all the excited chat about wheel-phlanges and wheeltappers, if one strained one's ears above the sound of jabbering train-spotters, and the accompanying rustle of greaseproof-clad tomato sandwiches and Thermos flasks of stewed tea, rumours can be heard.

Having an abiding interest in what happens in the fair county of Derbyshire, particularly with an eye to a decent blackmail in lieu of a personal pension plan, I made notes. Later that evening, having divested myself of the brown trenchcoat and the fedora, I slipped in to the Hollybush Inn, just down the road at Grangemill, and made a few discreet enquiries.

When a stranger walks in to a country pub, and starts asking questions in a "furrin" accent, the locals clam up. How to succeed? There were two options. Number one, go out and buy a pair of big boots, a woolly hat, anorak, big red socks and a couple of ski poles, because this particular hostelry is popular with walkers from all over the country, and one would blend in with the crowd, provided that one was prepared to eat the odd cheese and onion sandwich, for the sake of authenticity.

The other method was to keep buying beer for one of the locals. Not much of a choice, you would say. Boots, £79.95. Socks, £8.99. Jacket, £49.99. Poles, £15.06. Map, £13.99. Waterproof Map Case, 29.99. Woolly Hat, a fiver. Total, £229.97. Frankly, that seems a tad steep for a bit of gossip that may or may not be fruity enough. Obvious answer. Have you ever tried to get a Derbyshire countryman sufficiently inebriated that he will talk freely? Ask him if he fancies another pint, and suddenly Bert and Harry and Charlie and Stan and Fred all materialise out of the shadows, pints are accepted and they disappear back to where the spiders lurk. In addition, each and every one of them has a capacity for liquid that remains unequalled, even among the more successful breeds of camel. Bert, Harry, Charlie, Stan, Fred and also Young Jim and Ar Kid, who came in later but still managed to shift a fair bit of liquified hops and barley, cost a quid or two.

Mind you, I got there in the end. When it looked as though the odd eye was glazing over slightly, I chanced to mention Elizabeth Ann.

"Ar, she be a fine filly. She got the best legs this side of the Pennines, an' no mistake."

Hello, I thought. We're getting there. I asked what her relationship with Howard might be, for Howard was, I had heard a contender.

"She'll walk all over 'im, sure as eggs."

"I hope she isn't wearing high heels!" I quipped. Silence. Then Young Jim glanced across at Fred - or Stan, I couldn't see that well, by this time.

"You're not confusing her wi' Squaw's Fella, are you?" he asked, a strange smile playing about his lips.

"You're not telling me that there are native Americans involved in all this? It's truly transcontinental!" Somehow, saying 'transcontinental' was more difficult than usual.

"Tell ye what, Sirrah," said one of the older men, nodding at the barman, who began filling pint pots, "tek this bit o' paper, but don't read it till tomorrow morning, or it won't help."

With a swivel of the hips that belied his advancing years, he handed me a piece of tantalisingly warm paper, took a fresh pint from the proferring hand, sank it in what seemed like only seconds, and left. I sat back and closed my eyes, for only a second. When I opened them, the place was empty; just the landlord, washing hundreds of empty glasses. He very kindly filled in the cheque for me, I didn't seem to have enough cash, and my hand was shaky. Maybe I was going down with something. I left, got in to my car, and fell asleep.

When I woke, the following morning, I set off for Matlock, hoping to find somewhere that sold hot coffee, a bite to eat and aspirin, not necessarily in that order. Suddenly, as I drove down the Via Gellia towards Cromford, I remembered the bit of paper. I pulled in to the bus stop just before the traffic lights, opposite the bakery, and felt in my pocket. I pulled the crumpled scrap out of my jacket and tried to remove the creases. Trying to read crumpled paper with crumpled retinas is never easy.

Pikehall Harness Racing, competitors list. Horses: Levi Joe, New York Sweetheart, Another Man, Elizabeth Ann, Howard's Contender. In a daze, I drove on, and got a coffee and a bacon sandwich. Fine, I thought, I shall have to find out more, now that I have come this far.

Visions of an early retirement faded like the morning mist on the Derwent. I read further. Harness racing is a sport whereby the horses pull a kind of lightweight, one-man chariot-frame. Trotting means that the horse may not break in to a canter but must go no faster than a trot, although it seems that this is still a fair pace.

Of course, it isn't that simple; if it was, it wouldn't be worth having a British Harness Racing Club, which is like the Jockey Club, with wheels. There are two forms of pace, either the trotter, which involves the horse's legs moving forward in diagonal pairs, or the pacer, whereby the legs move laterally, in that the right front and the right hind move together, and then the left front and left hind.

Not many people know that horses can tell the difference between left and right, but there you are. The chariot thingy that they pull is colloquially known as a bike, which is misleading in that the wheels are either side rather than in line, although the horse doesn't know this. It is at that end of the beast that cannot see. The official name is a sulky, which presumably describes the state of the horse in not being able to see rearwards.

I needed more time to absorb this information. I ordered another coffee, and a sausage cob. A cob is a breed of horse in some places, but in Derbyshire it means what Sheffield calls a breadcake, but Barnsley refers to as a plain teacake. I need hardly mention that this is known in Lancashire as an oven-bottom muffin, or further south it might be a bun. Or a roll. Or a bap. It matters not what you call it, it goes perfectly with a tube or two of what had once been pig.

I consulted my paper. The races take place twice a year and one of these events was due soon. I resolved to go. Unfortunately, I never made it. It goes without saying that you don't get in for nothing; there are trophies to pay for, loudspeakers, rent, all that sort of thing. I consulted my bank balance.

Fortunately, I am not a betting man, indeed, I have never been inside a betting shop, since I refuse to believe that a horse will try harder merely because my five quid says it will win. Horses don't think like that, they've got all on trying to remember to put their left front foot forward at the same time as their back left. Nobody ever said it was easy being a horse.

Anyway, I couldn't have afforded to put a bet on, even if I had wanted to. For some reason I can't yet fathom, my account is short exactly £229.97p. Odd, that!

Stainsby Festival

For the first time ever, you start to realise that Derbyshire is actually a world leader, a trend-setter, a pioneer. Woodstock, indeed!

WHEN you see the names Edward II and His Worship and The Pig conjoined, it is only natural to be suspicious. When the moniker Flossie Malaville then crops up, the imagination runs wild.

What happened, leading up to the dastardly deeds of 1327? Where was Piers Gaveston, who was ever so slightly friendly with the monarch? Was this the Pig, although, being from Gascony, you would have thought that such a name was a tad inflammatory? Where did this perishing Snapdragon fit in, did it get bunged in the Crucible that was mentioned on the next line? Evenfurthermore, what had all this got to do with either Derbyshire or Glastonbury.

Glastonbury is a quiet little village in Somerset, a bit inland from Weston-super-Mare. It is best known for becoming a sea of mud for several days each year, when lots of people who are obviously masochists go there to listen to music which you could probably hear in Burnham-on-Sea. They live in inadequate tents, share sanitary facilities with thousands of like-minded lunatics, live on an unremitting diet of burgers and beer (which doesn't improve the aforementioned facilities), go slightly deaf, get a cold and then return home to spend weeks telling everybody how wicked/cool/brilliant/awesome/wow/like/man it all was.

This is a tradition. It seems that the people of Somerset welcome this event, especially if they own Portaloos or burger vans. The rest complain about the traffic and the noise. It has, they say, been going on for quite long enough now.

Derbyshire was way ahead. It may well be largely rural, as indeed is Zummerzet, where the Zyder Apples grow, but, me duck, it is also progressive. It had its own music festival ages before Glastonbury was even thought of. Well, a year anyway. For in 1969 Derbyshire reverberated to the merry music of the folk scene.

Now this is the point at which many will get a mental picture of some bearded wonder in a chunky-knit sweater, corduroy trousers and big boots singing in a nasal whine, with a finger stuck in his ear. Regrettably and unfortunately (a) some of them still exist and (b) on this occasion we are wrong, you and I.

There are very few of such people now, probably because they have had so many empty beer bottles thrown at them that they have, after a gap of a quarter of a century, eventually got discouraged, and moved to Somerset. It took that long because anybody who would sing down his nostrils with a digit in the ear-'ole is probably not going to be that sensitive, and thought it was some ancient rite. Rong! In point of fact, the folk, roots and acoustic scene is not only alive but flourishing, and there is some superb music. From bands like His Worship

There will be those gentlemen reading this who will remember the era of the first Stainsby Festival and may even still have the floral flares

and the Pig , Edward II and Crucible.

One of the things that you may have noticed is that those in the home-grown music world, as opposed to the manufactured world of Pop Idol (Idle?) do not take themselves too seriously. Sure, they take their skills seriously, and the music that they are preserving for future generations, but they are not half as self-obsessed as so many of those that get air-time on Radio One.

If the Tabloid Press is true (hah!), then the world of popular music is rife with drugs and so forth. Folk musicians, and I have been out with a few of them over the years, consume beer. Usually very dark coloured beer, from breweries that the big chains have never heard of, and so much the better. These libations have names such as Land of Hop and Glory, Twist and Stout, Dark Side of the Moon and Sgt. Pepper's Stout, all of which, you will notice, have a musical theme. And before you ask, no, I am not in the employ of the brewery that makes these excellent beers, but it is a Derbyshire brewery, and I like them. So there. It's my book, and I can do what I want. It is Spire Brewery, in Staveley.

Originally, the festival was billed as a folk festival. but the word 'folk' has been dropped. Despite that, most of the music you will hear is acoustic and none of it will be enhanced by studio techniques - it is music as music was intended, especially if you are of a certain vintage.

Of course, there will be those gentlemen reading this who will remember the era of the first Stainsby Festival and may even still have the floral flares and the shirt with the massive collars in their wardrobes. If you still have the shades with lenses large enough to land a jump-jet on and the silvery platform boots, do not throw them away. You may well look faintly ridiculous in them yourself, but e'er long a member of the family will be invited to a sixties party, and you will be able to show them how groovy you were, when festivals were new.

Incidentally, it was in this same year that the first jump-jet, the Harrier, came in to RAF service. On April 1st, to be precise, and make of that what you will.

The same advice applies to the ladies. You might not want to wear that A-line mini-dress again, or the empire-line one, never mind the floppy hats, but you will earn mega respect for having had the nerve to wear them, much as you did the Capless Stretch Wig in various colours.

Also, and bear this in mind, you may very well have originally paid for some of this stuff with the very first 50p coins, when we still called it ten bob. If you have grandchildren do not try and explain it to them, despite having the clothes. They will only think you are some kind of dinosaur, especially if you tell them that this lot came from the same year as the first ever Miss Universe pageant, which, I am sure you will remember, was won by Gloria Diaz.

Inevitably, there are those who will tell you that the Grandaddy of all music festivals was Woodstock, which is every bit as famous because of the name of the little bird in the Snoopy cartoons. Wrong again. Woodstock was on 15 August 1969. Stainsby was in July, and not only that, a full month before the Beatles released Abbey Road and two months before colour telly hit Britain. For the first time ever, you start to realise that Derbyshire is actually a world leader, a trend-setter, a pioneer. Woodstock, indeed!

Tissington Well Dressings

He constructed a frame of wood taken from what had once been the outhouse, then he mixed mud to a glutinous consistency and started to stick all the petals he had gathered randomly in to it.

IN a mean, wattle and daub hovel just outside the Derbyshire village of Tissington, in the July of 1349, a cockerel crowed triumphantly to the morning sun. A scant four feet away, lying festering in sleep, was the reeking body of one Waryn the Serf, a genteel man who had been thrown out of the community some 25 years before, because of his pagan beliefs.

Now, he lived in the aforementioned hovel with its leaky roof and slightly odiferous walls, where he had used a little too much manure to swamp-mud in their construction. Beside him, under a flea-infested blanket, formerly the property of a horse, his wife Eagdyth stirred, sniffed luxuriantly, a brave move given the circumstances, and muttered, "Shut that thing up, will you?"

Waryn reached blearily out with a horned, work-calloused hand, and fetched the rooster a dizzying back-hander around the back of the head. It retired sulkily to the corner, muttering things that only poultry can understand.

Eagdyth sucked noisily on her last remaining tooth, delicately wiped her nose with the sleeve of her garment, that doubled as nightdress, working clothes, evening attire and Sunday best, coughed and spat with unerring accuracy at the rooster. It slunk out through the hole in the wall that the mice had originally excavated, as an escape route.

"Woss it like out there?" she enquired of her husband. He pushed the door open an inch with his foot and peered into the bright light of the early morning sun.

"Another flaming dry one," he mumbled, "I can't remember what rain looks like. Them frogs down the bog is so skinny, you can't get a decent breakfast off of 'em any more."

He rose, unsteadily, and staggered outside, contemplated the idea of a wash, discarded it almost instantly, and sat on a tree stump, scratching. His reverie on the state of the English economy, the supremacy of the Norman aristocracy over the home-grown variety, the price of manure and the unlikelihood of finding anything worth eating was interrupted by the rusty hinges of his wife's voice.

"What we in for today, then? Another exciting day down by the bog, being social lepers, not talking to nobody? Another boring day of picking fleas off each other and a plate of gruel at dinner? I can't wait?"

He gazed at her once-lovely face, now pock-marked with a myriad blackheads, yellowheads and assorted pimples.

"How the blazes should I know?" he snapped. "What d'you think I am, a perishing fortune teller?"

"Werl, you've got the chicken's entrails out there, can't they tell you nuffink? You're the one what keeps on sacrificing mice or rats to that pagan god of yours. You tell me, O omnipotent one. Can't you wave them skulls about a bit, chant a bit louder, all that? We can't carry on like this."

She attempted to toss her grease-laden tresses, which fell lank to either side.

"Leave it with me, I'll think of sunnink," he said, unconvincingly, and set off in the hope of finding a tasty, plump hedgehog, or a brace of voles. The problem is, he mused, there's not much in the way of industry around here. There's no coal, no copper, no iron, railways haven't been invented yet, we're still messing around with bows and arrows rather than machine guns or other accoutrements of civilisation. I'd chuck myself in the river, only there's not enough water in there to drown a mouse, even if you could find one.

He sat moodily on the squelching, muddy bank of the stream - calling it a river was over-egging the pudding a bit, but a man needs dreams - stirring the stinking, grey clay with a stinking black foot. Overhead, a blackbird sang cheerily. He aimed a stone at it, which missed, but in its inexorable way to earth, despite the fact that Sir Isaac Newton was yet 230 years away, it hit a tall, flowering plant, dislodging several petals. They settled slowly in the gooey mud that Waryn had mixed, the colours vibrant against the grey, in the morning sun.

"And a fat lot of good that did!" snarled Waryn, despite the fact that even he was aware of the aural capabilities of the Yellow Waterlily (Nuphar Lutea) and the Himalayan Balsam, although he had never studied Latin at school. He had never studied anything else, either, since the only day that he went near the school building, he had been stoned as a health hazard.

He sat and gazed mindlessly at the coloured patches, when the seeds of an idea germinated in his tiny little mind. If the locals wouldn't even go near him - Black Death was a real risk - at least they would look at his work, especially if he could surround it with a bit of mystique. He hurried back home, his knuckles barely scraping on the ground.

"A dirty great wooden frame, full of mud, with flower petals stuck in it to make a picture? You want your bumps feeling, mate!" said Eagdyth, lovingly.

Undeterred, Waryn set to work. He constructed a frame of wood taken from what had once been the outhouse, until it fell down in the terrible gales of 1342. Then he mixed mud to a glutinous consistency, almost exactly like his wife's porridge, and started to stick all the petals he had gathered randomly in to it. Eagdyth came nearer, and peered myopically at her husband's labours. He grinned a toothless grin, and said the immortal words "Can you tell what it is yet?".

"Looks like an octopus to me," she replied "Not that I know what one is, mind, but that's what it looks like."

Write a notice that it's to ensure pure water, and bolt a collecting box to it. Years from now, they'll be lapping this up

"Good. Adds a bit of mystique, a bit of mystery, a bit of.... what's the Norman for 'Je ne sais quoi?'"

"I don't know, but what d'you want mystery for?"

"Werl, I was going to sneak up in the night, bung it by the well, you can write a notice that it's to ensure pure water, and bolt a collecting box to it. Years from now, they'll be lapping this up, they'll be making pictures of men flying to the moon, they'll never even know it was a pagan what started it.

"There'll be coaches coming from Cambria, and Scotia and other parts of Brython, never mind the Goths and the Vizigoths and the Huns and loads of other foreigners."

Eagdyth sniffed again, eloquently.

"You're mad," she said, "but it's worth a try!"

Tunstead Dickey

What Health and Safety would have thought is anybody's guess, but Ned's dead head stays in bed.

IT is a reasonable bet that Solomon never visited Derbyshire, and there are those cynics who will tell you that this is because he was the wisest man that ever lived. Take no notice of them, this is merely jealousy.

Despite his never having been here, he has a Temple named after him, just south of Buxton. How impressed the man himself would have been is a subject for conjecture, for it is only about 20ft tall, and about 11ft in diameter, a simple tower with nothing inside it but a spiral staircase and a good view at the top.

The original temple, in Jerusalem, was rectangular, and about 150ft by 75ft. (Actually, at risk of bursting the bubble, ours was named after one Solomon Mycock, who built it in 1895, but we can conveniently overlook that fact).

It contains no Most Holy, no Altar of Burnt Offering, no Menorah, or lampstand, no gold-covered cedar of Lebanon, in fact, it is a pretty pale imitation. Not many people seem to flock there for worship, either. However, Solomon (the original one, not the 19th century publican) did leave Derbyshire something extremely interesting, although it is not exclusive to the county. It is his writings in the Scriptures, not the least of which is the book of Ecclesiastes, meaning, literally, the Congregator.

Amongst other things, he tells us, and with the greatest of authority, at chapter nine and verses five and six, "The living are conscious that they will die; but as for the dead, they are conscious of nothing at all, neither do they any more have wages, because the remembrance of them is forgotten. Also, their love and their hate and their jealousy have already perished, and they have no portion anymore to time indefinite in anything that has to be done under the sun."

A scant four verses later, so as not to leave us in any doubt, he tells us: "All that your hand finds to do, do with your very power, for there is no work nor devising nor knowledge in the grave, where you are going."

Considerately, he then goes further, in telling us that there is a same eventuality as respects mankind and the beast. As one dies, so the other dies, that they all have one spirit, and there is no superiority of man over the beast, when it comes to snuffing it. This can mean one of two things - either, when you're dead, you're dead, or, there is a risk that, if, as many believe, you are on your way to an Elysian cloud, a pair of wings and a harp, you might well bump in to the very lamb that provided last night's tea, which would mean a bit of very fast talking indeed. It could be highly embarrassing.

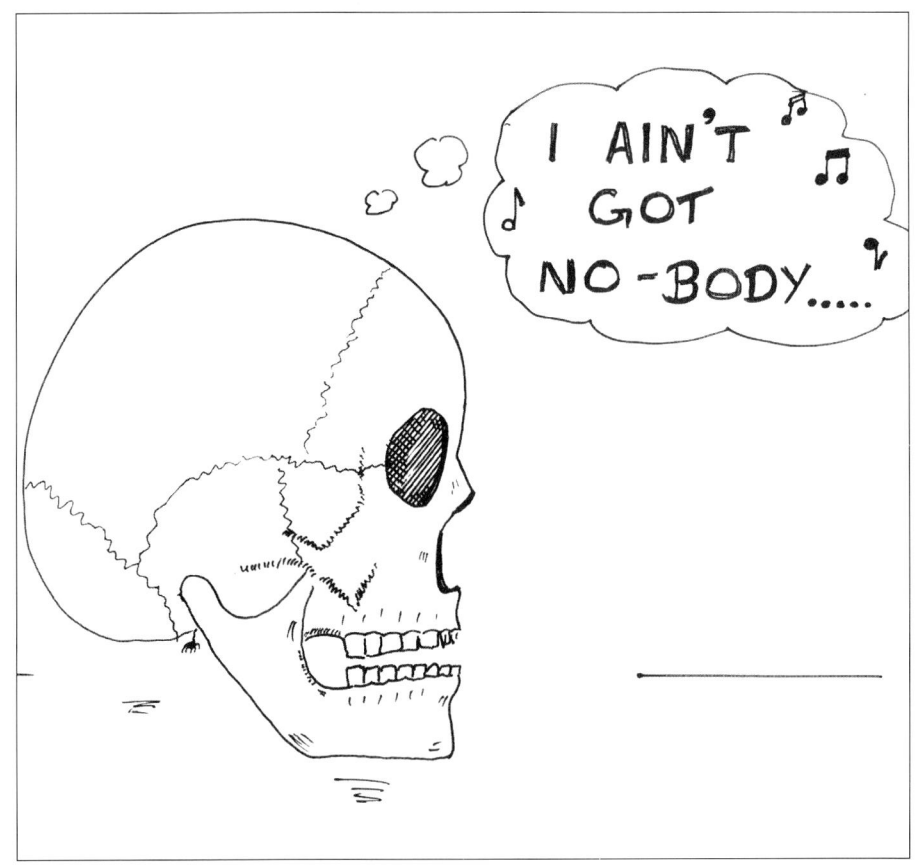

How a skull, without the requisite bits and pieces, can scream, or why it should choose to do so, in such a tranquil area, is not known

Despite all this, such legends as Tunstead Dickey, or Dicky, possibly Dickie, he doesn't appear to be fussy, persist.

The erstwhile Mr Ned Dixon, for such was his soubriquet, was a gentleman, formerly resident at Tunstead Farm, near Tunstead Milton, but now deceased. That doesn't mean he has left the building, though, for rumour has it that he, or at least that portion which was his head, is still around.

The story goes that he was a-returning from the wars, in the early 19th century, and was done to death, presumably in a dastardly manner, in his own bedroom, which his upper regions have never left. What Health and Safety would have thought is anybody's guess, but Ned's dead head stays in bed.

Alternatively, it is the ghost of a woman, and since it has been described as a "Screaming Skull", this seems more plausible. How a skull, without the requisite bits and pieces, can scream, or why it should choose to do so, in such a tranquil area, is not known, but no matter who she is, what she did, why she shuffled off this mortal coil or why she has chosen to hang around in such an alarming manner is unrecorded, which makes all the best stories even better.

This doesn't actually fit in with tales of hob-nailed boots thumping about in the attic, scythes being whetted, and the clatter of hay-making implements and other tools, but since they were told by farm workers who may have imbibed a quantity or two of the foaming brew before retiring, this may go some way to explaining things.

But then, Shock! Horror! It was discovered that things had gone a bit quiet, and Dickie himself had been nicked. Quite why anybody would break in to a remote farmhouse and steal a smelly old skull is beyond imagination, which is already stretched to the limits. To stretch it yet further, Dickie was, by felon or felons unknown, returned to his old haunts, where he seems to have been a bit of a pain in the neck. He has since disappeared yet again, only this time, he has been forcibly ejected, by whom we know not.

It is always possible that he was stuffed in the wheelie-bin, and is currently trying to work out some means of exit from the landfill site he currently inhabits. Or, to make such a suggestion, would one need to be off one's head?

So, is there any way of ever finding out what really happened at Tunstead Farm, all those years ago? Not a ghost of a chance.

Weston-on-Trent Scarecrows

Scattered around the village, immobile, and therefore more than a bit scary, are a myriad strange people, like some science fiction film, frozen in time.

THERE are very few crows that dare go anywhere near the village of Weston-on-Trent, and those that do go in disguise.

Weston-on-Trent lies, not on the River Trent, as the name implies, but merely relatively close to it. This level of confusion is traditional in Derbyshire, which, much like Cornwall, is the sort of place where somebody will tell you that a certain village is a mile away, and it turns out to be three-and-a-half. It is about six miles from Derby as the crow flies, but, as was ascertained earlier, few of them dare risk it. Why is this? Fear. Pure, simple, unadulterated, abject fear.

You would be forgiven for thinking that South Derbyshire has a latter day Flak Battalion, that takes pot shots at passing birds, but this is not so. Not yet, anyway, although rumours are afoot that it has been suggested in certain quarters, and Oerlikon, the world's biggest manufacturer of anti-aircraft guns, are expecting the order to drop through the letter-box any day now.

What terrifies masses of Corvus Monedula, Corvus Corone and Corvus Frugilegus is not the worry of cordite and splinter, for they are all remarkably agile birds, and dodging an ascending 35mm shell is child's play, they can see it coming from miles off, they have eyes like a hawk. No, it is the stationary figures, dressed in all kinds of strange costumes, arms outstretched, that induce panic.

The crow is a brave bird, and manoeuvrable, but it's intellect is in almost direct inverse proportion to its valour. To put it another way, they are as thick as a brick, although bricks do not fly well.

Scattered around the village, immobile, and therefore more than a bit scary, are a myriad strange people, like some science fiction film, frozen in time. Solitary police officers point radar guns at non-existent motorists, mechanics lie underneath the cars that the Old Bill are waiting for, firemen rescue cats, whilst assorted superheroes rescue humans, the Simpsons watch a silent television, as do a family, ranging from baby to Grandma.

Elsewhere, a plumber appears to be attempting suicide by flushing himself down the loo, witches watch, cackleless, as dinosaurs prepare to roam the county once more, if only somebody would breathe life in to their bodies of straw.

At the top of the village, a busty American country singer struts her stuff, looking for all the world like Dolly Parton. Presumably a corn dolly. In amongst this disconcerting array, under blue and crowless skies, roam everyday people, doing everyday things, such as

107

making Wallace and Gromit keep silent vigil over those places where, before the semis were built, fields of grain would have ripened in the sun.

Of course, there is an aim to this, other than amusement, in that you can buy a Scarecrow Trail map (for folding money) and follow along, answering questions as you go. Questions on a printed sheet, that is, the scarecrows themselves don't ask you anything. Yet. Mind you, it feels like it is only a matter of time.

This isn't an old tradition as such, having only been going for a relatively short period, but it seems pretty certain that it will be around for a long time to come. There are other Scarecrow Festivals in any number of Derbyshire Villages, amongst them Ticknall, Crich, Holymoorside, Coal Aston, Barlow, Bradwell and Tansley.

During the Second World War, various camps were built near Weston, for the Army. In the 1980s, one was being used by the Ukrainian Youth Association for whatever it is that Ukrainians get up to in Derbyshire. In 1980, during the build-up to the Moscow Olympics, Weston-on-Trent was named by the Soviets as being a centre of international espionage, as they claimed that "Anti-Olympic Agents" were being trained there, by, of all people, the CIA. Makes you wonder what they were so scared of!

This isn't an old tradition as such, having only been going for a relatively short period, but it seems pretty certain that it will be around for a long time to come

Wetton Toe Wrestling

All you will need, other than a sense of humour and a pint or two, is to know the difference between the two competitors and be able to recognise the starting cry of 'Toes Away'

THE people of Wetton are not happy, and for good reason. Amazingly, it has nothing to do with local taxation, nor local government, nor yet that the prices have gone up at Ye Olde Royal Oak Inn, a first-rate establishment that deserves its good name, it being over 400 years of age. It serves a fine pint of Abbott Ale, which is another example of the close co-operation of church and boozer.

Derbyshire is full of similar places, such as the Church Inn at Youlgreave, and herein lies the problem. Not the perennial one about temperance, but quite the reverse, since the clergy have long made parishioners thirsty with lengthy sermons, and snoring is known to give you a dry throat.

If we look at the beginning of the Royal Oak's history, it is a moot point as to who would have been first to the bar for a swift one before the roast beef of Olde Englande, preacher or preachee. You see, Wetton is often thought to be in Ashbourne, since that is its postal address, but officialdom is telling us geographical porkies, for Wetton lyeth not in Derbyshire but in Staffordshire. This can be important, even to the casual visitor, since no-one has ever yet encountered a Derbyshire Bull Terrier, or, more pertinently, Derbyshire Oatcakes.

Staffordshire people are a proud race, having endured a total of nine boundary changes since 1844, when the Royal Oak was still pretty Olde, never mind their own castle and the Staffordshire Knot. To suddenly be dropped into Derbyshire when you least expect it is a shock to the system. Indeed, it can give you a bit of a jolt when you are expecting it, but that's for another day.

Wetton, for the less well-travelled amongst you, is the home of one of the world's more extreme sports. Not, as you would imagine with all those hills and cliffs around, bungee jumping, or throwing yourself off a convenient ledge with only a nylon sheet and an old bicycle frame to keep you in the air, but far more exciting.

"Inna Blue Cornah, weighing in at about 3oz, the current world champion, ladeez an' gennelmen, we give you, the Big Toe of.... Alan 'Nasty' Nash." Imagine, if you will, across the great divide between the contestants that afficionados call the toedium, sits, unshod, former champion Paul "Toeminator" Beech. Battle is to be joined, as it has done since some time in the 1970s.

At any great sporting event, the atmosphere is all. Go to any major sports arena, whether it is Madison Square Gardens, the Millenium Stadium in Cardiff, Wimbledon, even your local cricket club, and you will inhale the liniment, the sweat, warm leather. Anxiety is in the air like the acrid stench of zebras. The smell of money is at the fore. It was no different at Ye Olde Royal Oak, except that there wasn't much in the way of leather, but another, perhaps more invasive odour. It may, to be fair, have been something to do with the excellent food served by mine host, there may have been a good Camembert on the menu that night, mayhap a gorgonzola or two, or perhaps it was merely over-active imagination.

The smell of money, the big bucks of the world light heavyweight bout, the fiscal excesses of the Football Association, the passage of folding stuff at the Cesarewitch is replaced by the smell of bitter beer. The stage is set!

And then, it all fell apart. For reasons that those in the village will only discuss behind closed doors, and that after a thorough search for bugging devices, the championship, the jewel in Staffordshire's crown, was ripped from them and taken, I like to imagine kicking and screaming, over the nearby border to Derbyshire; to Ashbourne, no less.

Derbyshire already has Chatsworth, Haddon Hall, Hardwick Hall, Renishaw Hall, Bolsover Castle, the Museum of Childhood at Sudbury Hall, Derby Gaol and the Royal Crown Derby Museum. It has the culture of Buxton Opera House, the splendour of the Rolls Royce Museum, the candyfloss and souvenirs of the Heights of Abraham, even, you might argue, Derby County Football Club. Why does it need yet more customs, more action-packed thrills, more spectacle, more attention?

The reason is simpler than you might think. You see, Derbyshire also has Kinder Scout, Dovedale, Mam Tor, Matlock Bath (especially if you own a Harley Davidson), the Crooked Spire, Monsal Trail, Longshaw and many other places that are, frankly, oversubscribed.

Go to any of the above, especially if there is that faint, yellowish thing in the sky that we laughingly call the sun, and you won't be able to park, much less get out of the car and walk. If you go on public transport, once you get off you will be reduced to that peristaltic shuffle that we all know so well, as the crowd moves at a snail's pace, trying to shove those who have already failed to see the local attraction due to the heaving mass of humanity covering it, and are making their disappointed way home, via a chip shop with a three-mile queue and a one-and-a-half-hour wait for a piece of greasy cod.

Toe Wrestling, and it deserves those capitals, does none of these things. You will not need chunky boots and big red socks, you will not need the walking sticks that look like you lost your skis on last week's trip, you will never require the hooded anorak and the maps in plastic covers, which would convince any roving Martians looking down at us on a weekend, that this is how all humans dress around here.

All you will need, other than a sense of humour and a pint or two, is to know the difference between the two competitors (admittedly different coloured nail varnishes would help, but this area is proud of its macho image) and be able to recognise the starting cry of "Toes Away".

The aim, purely and simply, is for the two protagonists to interlock big toes, and try to force their opponent's foot sideways on to the floor, much like arm-wrestling, but without the tattoos.

There are actually official rules, which can be found on the website of the Bentley Brook Inn in Ashbourne, that leave the cheat absolutely no toe hold. Contests must be of the same gender - none of this namby-pamby politically correct equality rubbish at the Bentley Brook - bottoms must be kept on the floor, similarly palms, but the unoccupied foot should be held in the air. Honestly, and this gave me untold pleasure, there will be three legs. The mental imagery is almost too much to cope with.

But the best bit, unlike in so many sports today, is the ruling on stimulants. No mention of such things as ephedrine, or clenbuterol, but then there is no need, for one particular stimulant is not just tolerated but encouraged. Alcohol. And this is the final piece of the jigsaw. There are, currently listed by the authorities, 29 breweries still operating in Derbyshire, from Spire in Staveley to Blue Monkey in Ilkeston. Shropshire lists 53, therefore it is only right that we all support another local, growing industry. After all, someone's got to foot the bill.

The aim is to interlock big toes and try to force your opponent's foot sideways on to the floor

Winster Pancake Races

If you happen to be staying there on Shrove Tuesday, you are more than welcome to join in the fun. As to whether you might win, well, that's a bit of a toss-up!

THE phrase 'Pancake Races' is, at best, misleading. In horse racing, horses are pitted against each other. Car racing has one car trying to beat another.

Running races, more properly known as athletics, involve a competitor trying to prove that he can run faster than anybody else there that day, even though they may have beaten him only a few weeks previously. He is then the Champion until someone else takes the title, who then relinquishes it in turn, and so on.

Somewhere, there is a man who can say that he is the fastest man in the world over, say, 100 metres. To those of us whose interest in athletics lies in watching it on telly, till the cricket comes on, this is a bit silly.

For example, do you know who the fastest man over 100 yards in 1957 was? No, nor do I, although, being sneaky, I just looked it up, and it was James Jackson, in 9.4 seconds. Look Mr Jackson up elsewhere, and you hit a brick wall. So much for fame.

Does this mean, then, that a Pancake called, let's say, Jack Jameson, rolled a distance of 100 yards in under 9.4 seconds? Not a bit of it, for pancakes do not roll. They need assistance, which is where the good people of Winster are unsurpassed.

Oh, there are pancake races, without the capital letters, in other parts of the country, such as the four held in London, or the events in Olney, Buckinghamshire, but these are not Pancake Races.

Pancake Races are held in Winster every Shrove Tuesday, which, since it is also known as Pancake Day, is no great surprise. The legend goes that a housewife, way back in the mists of time, was busy making pancakes one Shrove Tuesday, and had lost track of time when she heard the "Shriving Bell" summoning her and the rest of the sinful village to a bit of heartfelt confession. Forgetting what she was doing, in her panic she ran to church, still with pan in hand, and in her apron. Presumably her confession had something to do with getting boiling fat all over the vicar. It is unrecorded whether he finished up battered.

Notwithstanding the aforegoing, Winster has held Pancake Races for well over 100 years, during which time no vicar has been assaulted. The object is to run down the Main Street for a distance of about 100 yards, tossing your pancake as you go. There are various categories, obviously, because you wouldn't want to put a battle-hardened pancake veteran up against a mere toddler. He might trip up. Not unreasonably, the youngster would have a different sized pan, for it would be too much to ask of a four year old to carry a frying pan that weighs almost as much as he does.

*Pancakes do not roll. They need assistance, which is where
the good people of Winster are unsurpassed.*

There is scope for a handicapping system, whereby the more experienced athlete might have to carry a heavier pan, like those French ones that weigh about 4st each, and which let things become practically vulcanised to the bottom, but as yet this has not been implemented. Rumour has it that the Jockey Club is investigating.

Unlike the exclusive world of horse racing, or Formula 1, where you need the odd few million quid lying about just to afford the kit, the people of Winster are not elitist. If you happen to be staying there on Shrove Tuesday, you are more than welcome, apparently, to join in the fun. As to whether you might win, well, that's a bit of a toss-up!

Of course, a place like Winster doesn't just sit around for the rest of the year doing nothing, for it is more active than that. For a start off there are the Winster Guisers, but you already read about those ages ago, so we won't bore you with going over the same material again. Suffice it to say that guising and mumming are the same thing, the only difference being that one is easier to spell.

Mumming has been described as a show without reality, or a foolish ceremonial. This is not to be confused with displays of thousands of tanks, rocket launchers and flame-throwers being paraded through the streets of Beijing or Moscow, although there are obviously connections. The only suggestion is to go to Winster in December, and see for yourself.

There's plenty to witness in summer, too, though, so don't just go when it's cold, and when you'll appreciate gathering around a roaring log fire. In late June or early July, Winster holds its Wakes Week, or carnival week. High spot of this is the Winster Morris Men, one of the oldest troupes in the country, strutting their inimitable stuff, especially the Winster Gallop, outside the market Hall, smack in the middle of the village.

Not only that, but the crowning of the Carnival Queen, whist, quizzes, art shows, golf, football, traditional story-telling, rounders, chorus singing (Winster has several), the Hill Race, a Teddy Bears' Picnic, a duck hunt, a treasure hunt for those for whom ducks are a little mundane, a talent show, a barbecue, a fancy dress competition, a carnival parade, a tug-o-war, and of course, beer.

Sound like any other carnival anywhere else? Well, yes and no, most carnivals have at least some of the above, but few have all of them, fewer yet the Morris Men. And most amazing of all, for all that, Winster, a tiny little ex-mining town, has a population of only 633. Beat that!

Wirksworth Barmote Courts

The Barmaster was in effect the head honcho, although it is not thought that this expression was in current usage at the time.

DERBYSHIRE'S W. Michael Brooke-Taylor is a hero, and yet few have heard of him. Indeed, most will look at his surname, and say "Oh yes, I remember, Tim Brooke-Taylor, he was in The Goodies", and that will be it.

Those who know Buxton well will have seen Brooke-Taylor, Solicitors, on Terrace Road. So why is W. Michael, who, I am sure, will not mind if we are a shade more familiar, and call him Mike, a hero? Because he developed a marvellous system for reading ancient documents. This is only right and proper, in that he was at one time Barmaster to the Barmote Courts, as you doubtless knew.

Mr Brooke-Taylor's wonderful method of decipherment involved quantities of gin, vodka and rum. As he said in his own words, white rum, obviously. The amounts must perforce remain secret, for it would not do for any Tom, Dick or Harry to know what was writ in the sweet lang syne. The mixture was used in minute quantities to assist with the faded ink, the remainder being taken internally, which is the course of wisdom.

Of course, Mike, who was not Tom, Dick or Harry, had the advantage over most of the populace, in that he knew what the Barmote Courts were, and indeed, still are. They go back as far as 1288, and were originally formed to adjudicate in the customs and practices of lead mining, which was at one time the principal industry of the area around Wirksworth.

Lead has been mined here since the time of the Romans, from which we get the word "plumber" for one who dealt with pipe-work made of lead, Latin "plumbum". That is one of those facts that one learns at the age of 12, and nearly half a century later get the opportunity to use. Of such minutiae is all human life composed.

There were a goodly number of smaller courts, up until 1814, when the two main ones at Monyash and Wirksworth were combined, the latter hosting the affair up to this very day. Even to this day it is known as the "Soke and Wapentake of Wirksworth."

The area of jurisprudence is approximately 115 square miles, whatever that is in metric, but since it's been around over 700 years, this continental stuff is not going to have to matter.

The High Peak Mining Customs and Mineral Act of 1851 is rarely invoked these days, if only because the average apprentice plumber these days is largely going to work with plastic, but this was the pile of paper that ordained what the Barmote Courts would, or perhaps more accurately, could do. It regulated the giving of one-thirteenth of a miner's gain to the Crown, and one tenth, or a tithe, to the church. It judged on disputes within the lead-field, such as handing down punishments for taking water from the village's well to wash ore. In the 1670s, a fine of three shillings and fourpence was meted out for having raised heaps of soil near to fences, allowing the cattle to climb out.

The Court was composed of 24 jurors, the names of some still being recorded, the Barmaster and a Steward. The Barmaster was in effect the head honcho, although it is not thought that this expression was in current usage at the time. Certainly, in Roman times, the phrase was unknown, being more commonly called the Procurator Metallorum. He it was who ran the entire industry.

There was also the appointment of a representative of the Crown, the Monarch being entitled the Lord of the Field, which you could be excused for thinking came straight out of the pages of a JRR Tolkein novel. Their Majesties cannot make it every April when the courts are held, so they send a representative.

The life of our Royal Family is no sinecure, and there are always things that require their presence, for the cutting of ribbons, unveiling of plaques and the like. They must think that the whole country smells of fresh paint.

The courts are are a link with the very people that made Derbyshire what it is

The present Courts are held in the Moot Hall on Chapel Lane, in Wirksworth, in a building that was erected expressly for the purpose in 1814. There had been an even older Hall built in 1773, right opposite the Red Lion public house, which, if you want peace and quiet, and miners have never been shy and retiring, was a recipe for disaster, so they moved. However, two marble bas-reliefs were taken from the older Hall, and added to the newer one, which are still there today, in almost pristine condition. They contain the tools used in mining lead, such as the scales, pick and trough.

Even today, the Barmaster and 12 jurors meet with the brass measuring dish from 1509 in front of them. Better yet, they are also provided with bread, cheese, clay pipes and tobacco. Exactly what sort of baccy remains a mystery, and nor is it known if anybody avails themselves of a good smoke. All that we can say is, if you are going to have an ancient custom, do the job properly, none of this namby-pamby political correctness. If a juror, one of a dozen good men and true, wants a jolly good cough, then who are we to stand in his way?

Many of the items you see about the Barmote Courts tell us that appeal from the jurisdiction of the Courts is by Certiorari, which I need hardly tell you. As you will no doubt be aware, Certoriari is the present passive infinitive of the Latin verb certiorare, meaning to search. I apologise for going over such familiar ground, but there is always the remote possibility of someone who has never studied Classics, Latin and the Law reading this. Certainly, anyone who has even glanced casually at the works of Ulpian (170-228 AD), and particularly Ad Sabinum, will be cognizant of the aforementioned.

Hardly surprisingly, the Courts, both in Wirksworth, and another held in the Mechanics Institute in Eyam, have less to do than of yore, but they have a fantastic value. They are a link not just with men that loved a cheese sandwich and a good smoke, but with the very people that made Derbyshire what it is, and gave us much of the landscape we see around us. They are a symbol of the grit, determination and sheer hard graft that formed a county, and which can and still does display those attributes, if I'm any judge.

Wirksworth Church Clipping

*They don't do it because the Bishop
is watching, but because they want to,
for that is what old traditions are for.*

UNNOTICED in the cold, grey light of dawn, the messenger from the Bishop's Palace rode into Wirksworth, deposited the letter at the house of the parish priest, and continued on his dusty way. Some three hours later, the priest rushed out of the front door, his robes flapping around his legs, as he licked the last of a hurried breakfast of porridge from his wooden spoon, which he then tucked into the brown folds. He scurried to the churchyard, and confronted the foreman of the builders.

"Good Morrow, Master George. Prithee, hast thou nearly finished? The Bishop cometh right soon, late after this very noon, for to inspect the new building."

"Ey Oop, Parson," replied the foreman. "Ar, me duck, we just gotteth a bit of sweeping up and making good, and then we finisheth, and goeth on to the next job."

"I hath here a letter from His Lordship. He desireth on pain of death - yours, not mine - to know the exact dimensions of the new church, for taxes to levy. Hast thou them to hand?"

The foreman laughed, shortly, a laugh honed by forty years in the building trade.

"Thou jesteth, surely?" quoth he. "Ye plannes are yet with ye bosses in Derby. We hath not had ye dimensions for weeks, now."

The vicar shot a meaningful glance at the sun-dial in the church tower, the meaning being entirely lost on the foreman, if only because it was a normal summer's day in England, and whilst the sun might well have been blazing down at 35,000 feet in Business Class, down here it was failing dismally to get through six-and-a-half thousand feet of strato-cumulus.

"Then thou hadst better get them, and pretty pronto, or thou art right up the swannee!" he snarled. "Hast thou not got a tape measure?"

"Leaveth it out, mate, this is 1271, it hasn't been invented yet, we useth bits of string."

"Then picketh up thy string, and get measuring, else thou wilt feel the wrath of the Bishop, and he can get a bit on ye moody side, thou knoweth."

A small, scruffy mason with an unkempt beard in which crawled wildlife as yet unknown to science sidled up to the pair, on whom he had been shamelessly eavesdropping.

"What wantest thou, Wat?," asked the foreman.

"Werl, I gotteth an idea, that's all," grinned Wat.

"Er, what, Wat?" enquired the vicar.

"How tall art thou, pray, good parson?" snivelled Wat, obsequiously.

"Five feet, two hands and a thumb," snapped the parson, impatiently. "Why?"

"Each man knoweth his own height, yea verily. If each man here were to stand with arms outstretched, around ye church, we couldst add the heights together, and Bob ist thy Uncle."

"Why with his arms outstretched? Surely t'would be better if they lay, head to toe?"

Wat grinned evilly, and two unidentified beetles fell to an untimely death. "Wouldst thou want to put thy head near his feet?" he asked nodding in the direction of a plasterer, to whom the word 'Bath' was merely a town in Somerset.

"Well, head to head, then!" said the vicar.

"Thou art welcome to his lice, and if not them, thou canst do what they will with his verruca, the athlete's foot and the rest of it."

Wat rubbed his hands together, as if expecting a gift.

"Surely, Sir, thou knowest that the height of a man is equal to that of his arms length, and that wouldst giveth thou what thou needest."

"Forsooth, he's right," exclaimed the foreman.

"Wouldst it be better if ye men held hands?" asked the vicar.

"Not a snowball's, Guv!" replied Wat, quickly. Very, very quickly. "Union rules!"

"What?"

"Yes?"

"No, I meant, what art thou on about?"

"Just an idea I'm working on." said Wat, smirking.

The foreman looked around him, making a quick mental calculation of the amount of men available.

"Thou wilt never get round the whole church, with that lot," quoth he. "There are verily too few."

"Then just measureth half of it, and multiply by two. Ye building is symmetrical, thou knows."

The foreman looked hard at him, frowning.

"I'm a builder, not a mathematician. I can do adds and takeaways, but I never done them timeses and guzinters."

"Easy," replied Wat, more smug than ever. "I got an abacus in the boot of the horse."

"Eh?"

"'Tis a wooden horse, like what they had in Troy, which is south of here, somewhere near Lichfield, I think."

And so, all the building workers, the foreman and even the vicar and his wife stood around the church, arms outstretched, and told Wat what their height was. As they did so, a loud cough came from behind them. There, on a magnificent white horse, gilded Bible in his hand, was the Bishop. He watched quizzically, as all these people stood, tight up against the walls of the church, arms outstretched, and dismounted slowly, like John Wayne in one of the better films. He leant against his crozier, which he had taken from a saddle-bag.

"What goeth on here, pray?" enunciated the Bishop, very slowly.

"Good Day, my Lord," said the foreman, bowing low to the ground, and sweeping his battered hat from his matted locks. "It be an old Derbyshire custom, whereby all present do link hands and give the church a bit of a hug. It hath been done hereabouts for - ooh - ages!"

"And what dost thou call this fascinating custom, prithee?" asked the Bishop, impressed.

The foreman looked frantically around him, and caught sight of an elderly man, a pair of shears in his febrile hands, attempting unsuccessfully to make a piece of privet look like a peacock.

"Er, clipping, my Lord, Oh Revered and Reverend one."

"So, clipping the church, eh? Jolly goodeth. Keepeth it up then lads. Just one small question. Why in the name of all that's Holy, which includeth me, doth one see so many bottom cleavages on show?"

The foreman thought rapidly.

"We are a poor people, your Honour, and we cannot afford higher waistbands on our galligaskins, do it please you, Sir."

The Bishop smiled beatifically, nodded at the assembled builders and, taking the vicar by the arm, led him away, to be given a large meal. The vicar winked at the Foreman.

"Well done, my good man. Keepeth it up!"

And they have, every Easter, right to this very day. Of course, nowadays, it isn't just builders, but all the people of the village, and especially the children. They don't do it because the Bishop is watching, but because they want to, for that is what old traditions are for. Also, you very rarely see bottom cleavages these days.

Wat did his sums, and worked out the dimensions of the church. It was, at that time, 78 feet, two hands and a thumb by 234 feet, one hand and two fingers, which figures he took round to the vicar, and was given a flagon of mead for his trouble. Sadly, it made his trouble worse, for he had been a heavy drinker full many a long year.

The height was worked out by using the Pythagoras Theorem, which the vast majority of schoolboys, certainly in the mid-twentieth century, struggled with. That being the case, there is no point in spoiling your fun, and you are left to work it out for yourself. Your education will not have been in vain.

There are, of course, many people that will try and tell you that Clypping, or Clipping the Church, is an ancient Pagan festival, but it seems a bit far-fetched. They will also try and convince you that the word is derived from the ancient Anglo-Saxon word "clyppan", meaning to clasp, or embrace. Again, this is hard to imagine.

If, in your peregrinations around the County of Derbyshire, you should come across such unscholarly adumbrations, please point those who are so sadly misinformed in the direction of this book. They will only be grateful.

Miscellaneous Traditions

The colliers would not look down upon ladies who carried out this woolly work, but more often than not, it was done by the men.

SHOULD this section be about miscellaneous traditions, or traditional miscellany? Is there a difference, and if so, how miscellaneous is that, and is it therefore worthy of inclusion? The answer to both questions is "probably", or, alternatively, "probably not".

Truth to tell, it doesn't matter, it is just that there are little snippets of information that do not warrant a whole heading all of their own. It wouldn't be beyond the bounds of possibility to write a couple of thousand words on each, admittedly, but it might not be as interesting as the Editors had originally intended. You might get restive, start to shuffle about in your seat, maybe even put the book thoughtfully on the shelf, behind that one on cricket that you've been meaning to read for years, but never quite got round to.

To lessen these risks, we have left a kind of Spatchcock Supplement, which will, publishing being the item it is, have a huge great space at the bottom, where you can write your own notes, or maybe a rude comment or two. Any further information would be gratefully received, but any insults would only upset somebody, and it is maybe best to let sleeping dogs lie. The very worst is, they might dribble on the carpet.

South Normanton was known for its mining and its framework knitting. If you were a big, hairy, roughy-toughy miner, who spent twelve hours a day hacking bits of coal out of a tunnel in which you had to bend double, where there was an ever-present risk of gas and explosion, the air stank, it was extremely hot, the roof dripped all over you and the only respite during the day was fighting off the rats as you ate your snap and drank your bottle of cold tea, it might just be possible to consider those who made a living framework knitting as being a bunch of softies.

This is pure conjecture, but highly likely. Now, it is reasonable to assume that the colliers would not look down upon ladies who carried out this woolly work, but more often than not, it was done by the men. "Men? Nay, lad, bunch of pansies, more like. Tell thi' wot, we mun think of a disparaging name for them, sirree. What's tha reckon?"

"Nah then, Bill, ah've tekken notice that when we come up from t'pit, we're allus black, but we wash oursens, an we're back to reights ageean. Them lot, though, they sit theer on their idle (deleted) all day long, nivver brekking sweat, and they've all got shiny backsides (or something like that) to their trousers. We'll call 'em 'Shiners'."

So they did. Believe it or not, the Royal Air Force still uses a similar derisive name for those who make a living flying a desk. They call it Military Tradition. Quite right, too.

Knitting frames were also in use at Ashover, making items out of silk. It seems reasonable to assume that the machines were a bit on the noisy side, or the Health and Safety Inspector was a tad Mutt and Jeff, because the portion of the town that had most frames working in it became known as Rattle, a name the present-day hamlet still bears. Incidentally, an anagram for Rattle, Derbyshire, is "Sly, hardier, better," which is better than "artistry, beer held," but not half as funny as "blast thy derriere".

In an American publication called Popular Mechanics Magazine, May 1950, and costing the princely sum of 35 cents, appears a letter from a Major Eling-Smith, MC, of Borrowash. In it, he refers to an an automated shoe-cleaning machine, and what a superb idea that it is, but points out that the claims made about it have caused the good Major to be a bit peeved.

It seems that the magazine, which tells us amongst other things that it may well prove one day possible to fly to the moon, states that it was the custom of the wife to clean her husband's shoes. It transpires that Maj Eling-Smith made, in one short week, over 50 enquiries, and refutes this idea completely. Quite right too, and my wife agrees with me on this, but then, he goes on to say, "I would like to express my appreciation for your excellent magazine".

Doesn't it give you a warm glow, that a military man can disagree vehemently, but still say how much he appreciates a publication that is wrong. What went wrong? By the way, for those who hanker after the Good Old Days, in the same periodical there is an advert for the new, thrifty 1950 Studebaker, in disgusting yellow, which beats every other competitor, bringing in an economic mileage of 26.551 miles per gallon. Oh, and there is a brand of pipe tobacco that is so good, it stays lighted 19% longer, it burns cleaner by 16.4% and it has 21.6% less tar. In fact, the blurb tells us that it is so good, it is full of goodness. Traditional advertising nonsense?

Up until the beginning of the twentieth century (I still find it difficult to think of it as the last century), Black Marble was mined at Ashford-in-the-Water. You will read many articles telling you that it is not marble at all, but a highly polished dark grey limestone.

This is a load of mis-informed twaddle, which shows a complete lack of knowledge of what marble actually is. The Encyclopaedia of Geology says that marble is "a term applied to *any* limestone or dolomite which is sufficiently close in texture to admit of being polished". Still with me? It goes on to say that to an accurate writer, which hopefully includes Yours Truly, "the term is restricted to those crystalline and compact varieties of carbonate of lime, which when polished, are applicable to purposes of decoration." Quite simple, so far.

Black Marble is a form of limestone, or carbonate of lime, and it most definitely lends itself to being polished. A quick glance at some in, say, Chatsworth House, tells you that.

Ah, but we haven't finished yet! Whilst the splenetic dander is well and truly up, I shall continue, somewhat like a rampaging rhino.

"Perhaps the most generally useful marbles yielded by the carboniferous system are the black varieties, which are largely employed for chimney-pieces, vases and other ornamental objects. The colour of most black limestone is due to the presence of

122

bituminous matter... and the finest kind of Black Marble is obtained from near Ashford in Derbyshire". The horse has spoken. So, the most authoritative book on the subject says it *is* marble, but a few geeks on the Internet say it ain't. I know who I believe!

Whilst we are on about believing things that might or might not be true, nobody in their right mind would argue that Robin Hood was a real person, and he lived in Sherwood Forest. (That is one of those statements that says "If you don't not agree, you are not in your right mind, and you don't want to admit to that, ergo, Robin Hood was real.) There is also evidence that he came originally from near Hathersage, in Derbyshire. 'Tis said that Little John, his lieutenant, was from Hathersage, and is buried there. In the graveyard is the final resting place of a very large man who tradition says is Little John, or John Little, who, as anybody who is well-read will know (i.e. I just found out) was a nailmaker. By one of those strange quirks of fate, the grave is owned by the Nailer, or Naylor family. Therefore it is definitely Little John. QED. Let's face it, if it wasn't, how boring would all this be? Tradition also says that Robin, having been poisoned by Morgan le Fey, asked for his trusty longbow, and uttered his dying words: "Wheresoe'er this arrow landeth, bury me there."

He was the first man in history to be buried in the ceiling.

Conclusion

Instead of finding bucolic yokels in wellies, you may well come across a geography teacher, a metallurgist, a rock drummer, a cartoonist, a bus driver and a dental technician.

THERE are many popular misconceptions about the Peak District, many of them put about by such arcane bodies as Tourist Boards and the like, who have a vested interest in making any area look as though not visiting it would leave a massive hole in your life.

The general idea is for the browser of brochures to say to himself that, of all the places in the entire world, the Peak District is the one for him. Never mind that it is warmer in South Africa, booze is cheaper practically anywhere outside Britain, there are no beaches and the food isn't exactly exotic, there is no choice.

Of course, if you were to believe all the bumf printed on glossy paper, the whole area is inhabited by people who spend their mornings inspecting their sheep for the signs of Frothy Bloat and their afternoons milking Daisy, Buttercup and the rest of the herd. Lunches (dinners?) consist of bread baked that morning, a huge lump of cheese, an onion or two (pickled optional) and an apple. Evenings are spent in the local pub, still wearing the flat cap that is indigenous to the region, swapping hilarious stories about lead miners, healthful waters or the plague, whilst consuming vast amounts of cheery best bitter and eating pies.

Occasionally, amongst the brighter of the populace, the discussion centres around whether the health-giving waters prevented lead miners from getting the plague, thus allowing them to die early of lead-poisoning, making the whole thing more romantic.

Every single village has a well-dressing and a village idiot, complete with smock and a straw in his mouth. There will be a well-kept tearooms, a tiny souvenir shop, one or two of the more interesting cottage industries such as basket-weaving and a five-star restaurant, serving exotic foods at pre-1970 prices. It is idyllic. So idyllic, in fact, that the only other people that you will see, except perhaps the odd cove driving his horse-drawn waggon of hay, or farmers leaning idly on gates, looking into the middle distance, are visiting artists and poets.

The reality is, of course, somewhat different. Knock on the doors of a few cottages and instead of finding bucolic yokels in wellies, you may well come across a geography teacher, a metallurgist, a rock drummer, a cartoonist, a bus driver and a dental technician.

And sadly, not every settlement is steeped in a thousand strange traditions, incomprehensible to any outsider. Take, for example, the hamlet of Cross o' th' Hands, about ten miles from Derby. There isn't very much there, to be honest, but who cares? They've got the best name of any village anywhere in the country. Middle Wallop and

Little Snoring can't hold a candle to it, despite both having had airfields there many years ago. That is the only reason that Cross o' th' Hands is in this book. Because it deserves to be.

So does Brookbottom, if only because its main claim to fame is that it has one pub, one Methodist Chapel, one telephone-box but two street lights. Presumably this is so that should the Methodist, who is not accustomed to drinking, leave The Fox Inn in a state that the minister might not approve of, at least he can see his way to the phone box, to call for a taxi home.

Perhaps he would be best advised to move to Eggington, which has no pub at all, and it is forbidden, for some reason lost in the mists of time, to sell alcohol in the village. Probably not worth a visit for the confirmed bibulist.

You might not want to go to Doveholes, either, although it has quite a charming name. Doveholes was voted, in 2001, as being the Ugliest Village in Britain, and nothing much has changed since then. If you wish to see Doveholes at its best, drive through at night, preferably in rain or fog.

Botany Bay is well worth a visit, but not because you might see the very point where Captain James Cook landed in Australia aboard HMS Endeavour. Quite the reverse, really, because Botany Bay, near Coton In The Elms, Derbyshire, has been calculated as being the furthest point from the coast in England, being more-or-less 70 miles from Fosdyke, on the Wash. It has no special plantlife, so, what it boils down to is this. There is no botany worth mentioning, it is not a bay, but other than that it is worth recording. So it has been.

Equally important in the history of the Peak District is the village of Waldley, near Doveridge. In the year of our Lord 1994, the letter box fell over. That's it.

Whaley has an albino pheasant, Ambergate was known as Toadmoor and Bugsworth was changed to Buxworth, despite its Norman roots, on 13th April 1930, because the vicar didn't like it.

Birchover was rated in the Domesday Book as being worth eight shillings, or, in modern Monopoly money, 40p. Ashover was worth 30 bob, or £1.50. Monyash was recorded, at the same time, as being "A Place of Penal Settlement for Ill-behaved Monks".

You now know more than enough about Derbyshire and are qualified to travel the length and breadth of the county. You will be able to discuss what you know in the Snug or Lounge of any pub you come across. Do not hesitate to do so, for it is a sight more interesting than the plague, healthful waters and lead-mining. Honest.

Meet the Author

Suave, sophisticated, elegant, bon viveur, handsome. These are all adjectives that have never been applied to the compiler of this guidebook, Dafydd Manton.

Dafydd Manton

DAFYDD Manton has made it his life's mission to try and wring a laugh from the reluctant reader, such as yourself.

He started to lose his marbles when the RAF taught him the Morse Code and his entire world was made up of dots and dashes, prior to doing similar things in Russian and then German.

Dafydd initially fell in love with the Derbyshire Peaks from the cockpit of a Jet Provost training aircraft, on weather reconnaissance flights from Lincolnshire, which explains why he lives where he does.

He has an affinity with the quirky, the odd, the more unusual parts of life, and anything that will make him giggle.

He enjoys visiting Wales, where he gets the chance to speak Welsh and show off unashamedly. Nobody else can understand him.

A great fan of Rugby Union, having played at different levels for 22 years, it is unwise in the extreme to phone him if Wales are playing an international against England.

Dafydd lives at home with a monkey called Artaxerxes and a couple of other people.

• Dafydd Manton is a regular contributor to magazines in North Derbyshire and South Yorkshire including Active8, Dronfield Eye, Twist and Wings, all produced by Heron Publications Ltd.